MACMILLAN CULTURAL READERS

PRE-INTERMEDIATE LEVEL

COLEEN DEGNAN-VENESS

Italy

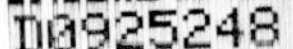

PRE-INTERMEDIATE LEVEL

Founding Editor of the Macmillan Readers: John Milne

The Macmillan Readers provide a choice of enjoyable reading materials for learners of English. The series is published at six levels – Starter, Beginner, Elementary, Pre-intermediate, Intermediate and Upper. The Macmillan Cultural Readers are a factual strand of the series.

Level Control

Information, structure and vocabulary are controlled to suit the students' ability at each level.

The number of words at each level:

Starter	about 300 basic words
Beginner	about 600 basic words
Elementary	about 1100 basic words
Pre-intermediate	about 1400 basic words
Intermediate	about 1600 basic words
Upper	about 2200 basic words

Vocabulary

Some difficult words and phrases in this book are important for understanding the text. Some of these words are explained in the text, some are shown in the pictures and others are marked with a number like this: [3]. Phrases are marked with [P]. Words with a number are explained in the *Glossary* at the end of the book and phrases are explained on the *Useful Phrases* page.

Answer Keys

Answer Keys for the *Points For Understanding* and *Exercises* sections can be found at www.macmillanenglish.com/readers.

Audio Download

There is an audio download available to buy for this title. Visit www.macmillanenglish.com/readers for more information.

Contents

The Places In The Book

Welcome to Italy

Population[9]: 61 million
Capital city: Rome (in Lazio)
Number of regions: 15 + 5 autonomous[10]
Autonomous regions: Sardinia, Sicily, Trentino-Alto Adige, Valle d'Aosta, Friuli-Venezia Giulia
Longest river: the River Po, 652 km
Number of lakes: 1,500

Italy is a country in Europe[1]. Today, about ninety-four per cent of the people in Italy are Italian, and most people speak the Italian language. But this has not always been true. The Italy we know today became one country only in modern times. Mountains cover two-thirds of Italy, so the people were divided[2] by their country's geography.

In 1861, Italy became one country when the different regions[3] joined together. Every Italian is proud[4] of their country, but they are even prouder of their region.

In the 1950s and 60s, Italy became internationally famous for design[5] and fashion, and continues to be today. But most of the cities responsible for Italy's financial success[6] are in the north. Turin is home to the Fiat car company, and Milan is Italy's centre of fashion. These two northern cities are the richest in the country.

An important part of any visit to Italy is seeing some of the Western World's most important art and architecture[7]. Much of Western culture began in Italy. There is also beautiful nature in Italy. It has got mountains, valleys, rivers, lakes, forests and beaches. Visitors go to Italy to enjoy skiing, climbing, walking, swimming and visiting the country's many music and food festivals.

Family is the centre of life for Italians. But football is almost as important as family! In fact, many people describe football as the country's national passion[8]. In Italy, there is something for everyone.

Warm-up Quiz

1 Which mountains cut Italy into east and west?
  a the Alps
  b the Apennines
  c the Pennines

2 Which volcano[11] is in Italy?
  a Mount Etna
  b Mount St Helens
  c Krakatoa

3 Where was ice cream first made?
  a Venice
  b Sicily
  c Naples

4 Who travelled to China in 1271?
  a Mussolini
  b Marco Polo
  c Hadrian

5 Who painted *Mona Lisa*?
  a Titian
  b Leonardo da Vinci
  c Michelangelo

6 Which man was an opera singer?
  a Ovid
  b Virgil
  c Pavarotti

7 What is a Stradivarius?
  a a violin
  b a piano
  c a guitar

8 Whose name was given to America?
  a Christopher Columbus
  b Amerigo Vespucci
  c John Cabot

9 What is the name of the Italian national football team[12]?
  a *Milan*
  b *Juvenal*
  c *Gli Azzurri*

10 What does Lamborghini make?
  a cars
  b pasta
  c shoes

1 Geography, Climate[13] and Environment

The Dolomite Mountains

Geography

Italy is a peninsula in the Mediterranean Sea in southern Europe. A peninsula is land with water on three sides. The Italian peninsula is about 1,130 kilometres long. It is the shape of a boot that is kicking a ball. The 'ball' is the Italian island of Sicily. Sicily is the largest island in the Mediterranean Sea. Sardinia is Italy's second largest island and Elba is the third. Seventy smaller islands in the Mediterranean Sea belong to Italy, too.

> 'Mediterranean' is a Latin word meaning 'in the middle of the Earth'. The Mediterranean Sea sits between Africa, Asia and Europe, with twenty-two countries along its coast.

Mountains

The Alps, mountains in the north, divide Italy from the rest of Europe. The northern regions of Piedmont, Valle d'Aosta, Lombardy, Trentino-Alto Adige and Friuli-Venezia Giulia share borders[14] with France, Switzerland, Austria and Slovenia. In these regions, there are groups of French-Italians, German-Italians and Slovene-Italians.

In the lower eastern part of the Alps are the beautiful Dolomite Mountains. The Dolomites are very different in shape and colour from the rest of the Alps. In the foothills at the bottom of the mountains there are many beautiful lakes. These include the five largest lakes: Garda, Maggiore, Como (one of the deepest lakes in Europe at 400 metres), Iseo and Lugano. Around these lakes are olive groves[15] and lemon and orange groves. Just south of the Dolomite Mountains is the Po Valley. Here farmers grow potatoes, rice[16] and wheat. Wheat is used for making bread.

The Apennine Mountains run 1,130 kilometres from the Cadibona Pass in the north, to Calabria in the south. This divides the country into east and west. These mountains continue on to the island of Sicily, making the mountains about 1,500 kilometres long. In the Central Apennines, east of Rome, is the highest part at 2,912 metres. This is called the 'Great Rock[17] of Italy'.

The western Alps are the highest mountains –
Mont Blanc: 4,807 m
Monte Rosa: 4,634 m
The Matterhorn: 4,478 m
Grand Paradiso: 4,061 m

'I'm from England but I've lived in Italy with my Italian husband and children for twelve years. We live in Florence, in Tuscany, so we enjoy the city's culture and the region's beautiful countryside. In summer, we enjoy a walking holiday in the mountains. I think Italy is the best place to live in the world!'

TESSA – AN ENGLISH TEACHER

Coast

Italy has nearly eight thousand kilometres of beautiful coast along the Mediterranean Sea. The Mediterranean Sea is divided into a number of smaller seas. The Adriatic Sea is between Italy and Eastern Europe, the Ionian Sea is to the south of Italy, the Tyrrhenian Sea is to the west and the Ligurian Sea is between Italy and the south of France.

Italy has beautiful sandy[18] beaches mixed with rocky coasts. The famous Italian Riviera is on the coast between south-east France and Tuscany on the Ligurian Sea. There visitors find lovely little villages, like Portofino. The west coast, from Tuscany to Campania, has long, sandy beaches. The coasts of Basilicata and Calabria on the Tyrrhenian Sea are rocky with some short beaches of white sand. Most of the Adriatic coast is flat and sandy so the beaches are very busy in summer. The coast between Trieste and Croatian Istria is rocky. Some of the most beautiful beaches are on the islands in the south.

Lake Como

Volcanoes

Between the Italian peninsula and Sicily is the Strait of Messina. From there visitors can see Italy's famous volcano Mount Etna. Etna is the highest active volcano in Europe at about 3,350 metres. South of Naples is the famous volcano Mount Vesuvius. Vesuvius buried[19] the towns of Pompeii and Herculaneum in AD 79 when it erupted. Stromboli is another volcano and one of the seven Aeolian Islands off Sicily. Stromboli is one of the most active volcanoes in Europe.

> i The word 'volcano' comes from the Aeolian Island Vulcano. This island gets its name from the Roman god Vulcan – the god of fire.

Mount Etna erupting

Climate

Most of Italy has a warm Mediterranean climate with hot, dry summers and wet winters that do not get very cold. But the summers in the mountains are short and not very hot. The winters in the mountains are long and very cold with snow. This is great for skiers. The Alps protect[20] Lombardy and Liguria from northern Europe's very cold winters, so winters in northern Italy are rainy but not cold.

In winter, the south stays warm because the sea brings warm air. Sometimes cold air from northern Europe travels south and brings snow to southern Italy's mountains. But people can continue to enjoy relaxing on the beach because the temperature is comfortable, at about 13°C in the daytime. Sicily gets about 2,500 hours of sun per year.

In summer, central Italy gets winds from Africa called Sirocco. This brings hot weather. In northern Italy the temperature can rise as high as 34°C in summer. In the south summers are even longer, hotter and drier with the temperature rising as high as 40°C.

Sicily has become drier and drier over the centuries because people have cut down trees in Sicily's central and south-western forests. Now there are only three forests in northern Sicily. This has resulted in less rain and dry rivers.

i

Inside the Italian borders are two enclaves. An enclave is a nation inside a larger nation. The first of these is San Marino on the north-east side of the Apennine Mountains between the regions of Emilia-Romagna and Marche, and the other is Vatican City in Rome.

Environment

Italy has made many positive environmental changes in the twenty-first century. It is working to make mountains safer for wildlife, the seas safer for sea life and the air in cities cleaner for everybody.

National parks

Italy's twenty-four national parks cover five per cent of the country. Here special laws protect the land and the wildlife. In the twentieth century, fourteen species[21] of animal in Italy became extinct – the animals were killed and the species no longer exists.

Stelvio National Park is the largest park in the Alps. It is in the regions of Lombardy and Trentino-Alto Adige. The park is home to many species of animal including red foxes, wild boar, chamois, ibexes and marmots, and to hundreds of species of bird including golden eagles. Over one hundred and fifty species of flora – plants and flowers – are found here, too. With glaciers and more than one hundred lakes, it is a wonderful place for walking, climbing and skiing. Cyclists in the *Giro d'Italia* cycling race[22] often prepare for it here. It is hard work cycling up Europe's highest mountain road – up 2,758 metres!

A glacier

An Apennine wolf

A Marsican brown bear

A chamois

A golden eagle

An ibex

A wild boar

A red fox

A marmot

As well as the National Parks, there are:

- 152 Regional Parks
- 147 National Nature Reserves
- 418 Regional Nature Reserves
- 30 Marine Protected Areas (places in the Mediterranean Sea where laws protect the sea and the sea life)

The Grand Paradise National Park was Italy's first park in 1922. It is in the Piedmont and Valle d'Aosta regions. It is full of high mountains, which were made by glaciers. The highest mountain is 4,061 metres. High in these mountains lives the ibex. The ibex was almost extinct in Europe so is now protected. Chamois, marmots and golden eagles are protected here, too. Visitors enjoy skiing in winter and walking here in summer.

In the centre of Italy is the National Park of Abruzzo. Here visitors can see mountains, rivers, lakes and forests. The park is home to sixty species of animal including the Apennine wolf and the Marsican brown bear. These animals were almost extinct but are now safe in the national park.

Environmental problems

Italians love their cars. This has made the air in cities unclean. In Milan in 2008, a new law made drivers pay to drive into the city centre. People who do not want to pay use buses or trains to get into the centre. Cities like Milan and Rome have bikes that people can hire to travel round the city. These things have helped to make the air cleaner.

Earthquakes[23]

Laws have helped to protect animals, plants and people but they cannot protect anyone or anything from earthquakes. Unfortunately, Italy has small earthquakes several times a year. In 2009 a big earthquake in Abruzzo killed 308 people. One of the worst earthquakes, in 1908, was in Messina and Reggio di Calabria. Over 72,000 people died. Fortunately, very dangerous earthquakes do not happen very often, and the small possibility of one does not keep tourists away.

Every year over forty million tourists visit Italy, and find a wide choice of geography to explore. And in the cities they find some of the world's most important treasures – architecture, art and history!

2 Cities and Architecture

The capital city, Rome

Rome

In Ancient Rome, the time before AD 476, writers called their city 'The Eternal City' because they believed it would be there for all time. It has two and a half thousand years of history, so it seems that they were right!

Rome is Italy's largest city and the country's capital. It sits on the River Tiber and has a population of almost three million people. It is a city of many treasures.

The myth[24] of how Rome was built

Romulus and Remus were twins – born on the same day. They were the sons of Mars, the God of War, and his wife Rhea Silvia. King Amulius wanted to kill their sons, so Mars sent them away. A female wolf gave them her milk so they lived. When they became young men, they started building a new town. But one day they argued and Romulus killed Remus. Romulus called his new town *Roma* (Rome) and he became its first king.

Architecture through the centuries

Name	Date	Example	Where
Classical	1st–5th centuries	*Arch of Constantine* AD 313	Rome
Romanesque	11th–12th centuries	*Siena Cathedral* (1136–1382)	Siena
Gothic	12th–15th centuries	*Basilica di San Francesco* (1228–53)	Assisi
Medieval and Early Renaissance	13th–14th centuries	*The Duomo Cathedral* (1420–36)	Florence
High Renaissance	15th–16th centuries	*Tempietto at San Pietro in Montorio* (1502–10)	Rome
Baroque	17th–18th centuries	*Gesù* (1568)	Rome
Neoclassical	19th century	*Galleria Vittorio Emanuele II* (1865)	Milan

Many visitors begin at the historic centre of the city. There they find the Pantheon, a Roman temple – a church – that has stood for almost two thousand years. The Ancient Romans believed in many gods, and in Greek the word 'Pantheon' means 'all gods'. But the Pantheon has been a Christian church since AD 608. Two kings, Vittorio Emanuele II and Umberto I, and the artist Raphael are buried there. The building is one of the most famous examples of Ancient Roman architecture and one of the most surprising. The first thing visitors see is daylight entering through a hole in the great dome[25] forty-three metres above them. This is called the oculus and is more than eight metres across. When rain enters, it quickly leaves through very small holes in the floor. It is one of the city's greatest architectural monuments[26].

Not far from the Pantheon are the famous Spanish Steps in the Piazza di Spagna. A *piazza* is a large public square. At the top of the steps is a French church and at the bottom is the famous Barcaccia Fountain[27], which is often seen in films. Tourists go there to meet friends and take photos. Then they go down via Condotti (*via* means road in Italian). Here they can find high-fashion clothes shops like Gucci.

Just a short walk from the Pantheon is the Piazza Navona, with its three beautiful Baroque fountains. It became Rome's marketplace in the fifteenth century. Palaces were built round the square for the pope and cardinals – important men in the Catholic Church. The Madama Palace was built in the sixteenth century for the powerful[28] Medici family. Today Italians go to the square to meet their friends in the cafés. North of the public square is the Roman National Museum[29], Palazzo Altemps. This museum has many wonderful classical sculptures[30]. To the south of this is the Museum of Rome. Here visitors learn about the history of the city since the Middle Ages – the time between the fifth century to about the middle of the fifteenth century.

East of the Piazza Navona is Rome's most famous fountain, the Trevi Fountain. This fountain has a sculpture of the god Neptune driving his chariot[31] through the water. For years, visitors have thrown money into the fountain because they believe it makes sure that they will return to the Eternal City. The money in the fountain is taken out and given to poor people.

The Trevi Fountain

The Capitol is on Capitoline Hill, one of Rome's seven hills. It was the centre of Roman politics[32] in ancient times and continues to be today. Visitors go there to see Ancient Roman buildings and monuments and to see the Forum below. The Forum was the centre of politics and law in Ancient Rome. It also had many important temples to different gods, including the Temple of Venus and Rome, built in AD 135.

Some Roman gods and goddesses

- Jupiter, god of the sky
- Juno, goddess of marriage
- Neptune, god of the sea
- Mars, god of war
- Venus, goddess of love
- Apollo, god of the sun, music and art

The Colosseum is one of the largest Roman buildings. It is a stadium that was built by the Roman king Emperor[33] Vespasian. It was finished in AD 80. Here gladiators – very big, strong men – fought each other, and men from the prisons had to fight hungry lions.

The Colosseum held about 55,000 people. The first gladiator games at the Colosseum were in AD 80. They continued for one hundred days and nights. Over five thousand wild animals were killed!

The Colosseum

'I'm proud of my city's ancient aqueducts with their beautiful arches. They have carried fresh drinking water to our city for centuries. Porta Maggiore carried two-thirds of Ancient Rome's water sixty-eight kilometres from the upper valley of Anio. Many modern cities today can't do that!'

CARLO – AN ENGINEER FROM ROME

Rome is famous for its Ancient Roman aqueducts – pipes and bridges that brought water into the city and carried water out. In Rome today, you can see the Porta Maggiore, Arch[34] of Drusus and Nero's Aqueduct.

Rome has more than nine hundred churches, but the most famous is St Peter's Basilica in Vatican City. Thousands of visitors go there every year to see Michelangelo's famous fresco[35] in the Sistine Chapel.

Florence

Florence, in Tuscany, is Italy's eighth largest city and one of the world's great artistic centres. Florence became a centre of art and culture in the Renaissance. Famous artists who lived and worked in Florence include Leonardo da Vinci, Michelangelo, Botticelli and Donatello. Today, crowds wait for hours to go inside the city's famous art gallery, the Uffizi. Here they can see some of the world's most famous paintings, including Botticelli's *Birth of Venus*.

Florence Cathedral is Europe's fourth largest church and the city's tallest building. From its orange dome, visitors can look out across the city. Inside are beautiful paintings and sculptures. The baptistery, the church building next to it, is the city's oldest building. It was probably built in the fourth century. The city's Piazza della Signoria is very large with sculptures of people from the city's history. It is a great place to listen to street music in the evening.

Florence's oldest bridge, the Ponte Vecchio, was built in 1345. It takes you across the River Arno. There you can find the Pitti Palace. The building started in 1458 for a banker called Luca Pitti. But by 1550 it belonged to

Florence

the powerful Medici family, and later to other powerful Florentine families. Today, visitors can walk from room to room inside the palace and see many wonderful treasures, including paintings by Raphael and Titian.

Outside Florence there are many smaller towns and villages that are also rich in history.

Pisa and Lucca

The Leaning Tower of Pisa

Pisa is where the River Arno meets the River Serchio. It was home to the Etruscans – the people who lived in parts of central Italy before the Romans. By the Middle Ages, Pisa was a rich and powerful town with a university. Probably no one goes to Pisa today without visiting the Piazza dei Miracoli. There, everyone takes photos of the famous Leaning Tower, the bell tower of the very large Romanesque cathedral.

Lucca is a beautiful medieval town. It has a 4,200-metre wall around it, which was built in the sixteenth century. In the past an Ancient Roman amphitheatre – a large outdoor theatre with no roof – stood on Amphitheatre Square. Lucca was the home of the famous Italian composer[36] Giacomo Puccini, who wrote the opera *La Bohème.*

Siena

One of the most interesting, probably Etruscan, towns in Tuscany is Siena. By the twelfth century, Siena was a powerful town and had fought many wars with Florence. With walls around the town that were built in the Middle Ages, Siena has lots of medieval Gothic architecture. This includes the beautiful cathedral. Inside the cathedral you can find wonderful art by Michelangelo, Donatello, Pisano and Bernini. Siena's famous festival, the Palio, is in the historic centre of the town every year on 2nd July and 16th August.

Venice

When visitors do not just want culture but also romance, where do they go? Everyone knows it is Venice, of course! With 118 islands and about 260,000 people, it is the capital of the region Veneto. Venice is famous for its water routes, called canals, and the Grand Canal has wonderful Gothic, Baroque and Renaissance palaces along it. Visitors have enjoyed riding on the famous gondolas – small boats – since the eleventh century. It is the best way[37] to see Venetian architecture.

Venice is famous for gondolas

Milan

> Since 1851, one city in the world is chosen every year to be the place for Expo. At Expo, visitors from around the world visit that city to learn about the country's culture, new ideas in technology and their ideas for the Earth's future. Milan was chosen for Expo 2015.

Not everyone goes to Italy just for its culture and romance. For people who like to shop till they drop[P], Milan is the place to go.

Milan is in Italy's richest region, Lombardy, and is Italy's second largest city. It is the centre of fashion and business, and is the country's financial centre as well. Milan's cathedral is one of the largest Gothic churches in the world at 157 metres long and 92 metres wide. In the north-west of the city is Sforzesco Castle, which was built for Francesco Sforza, Milan's new ruler[38], in the fifteenth century. From Sforzesco Castle you can see the Alps.

> Italy has forty-nine World Heritage Sites – places that belong to all people in the world. This is more than any other country in the world!

Italians from every region are passionate about their wonderful cities, ancient monuments, architectural treasures and beautiful countryside. But they are even more passionate about their food! From the number of Italian restaurants all over the world, it seems that Italians have one of the most popular cuisines[39] in the world.

3 Food and Drink

An Italian family eating together

Italian food is best when it is cooked by Italians in their own country. Eating outside with family and friends makes it taste even better. The Italian cuisine is healthy because it includes a lot of local fresh fruit and vegetables, fresh fish and meat, and local dairy products like cheese and milk.

The Slow Food Movement[40]

This movement was organized in 1986 in Turin by Carlo Petrini. He wanted to share his idea that local food, cooked well, is much healthier than fast food[41]. It is also one of the best ways to help local economies. The Slow Food Movement is now an international movement in 150 countries.

Mozzarella cheese

Olives

Polenta

Pasta

Tomato, mozzarella and basil salad

Meals

In Italy, the day begins with a small, simple breakfast, *colazione*. This is usually just a coffee and a small cake. Lunch, *pranzo*, is the main meal. This is eaten at home with the family when it is possible. Almost all Italians used to take two or three hours away from work to enjoy lunch and then have a rest. But this is changing in large cities. Workers may have only an hour, or less, for lunch and do not go home.

Buon appetito! is what Italians say at the start of a meal. It means 'good appetite' = 'enjoy your meal'.

'I love making polenta because it's one of my favourite dishes, and it's not complicated. In the north we eat more polenta than pasta. When you cook the polenta in water, you have to stir[42] it without stopping for about thirty minutes. My arm gets really tired but it's very important to continue stirring! When it's cooked, I leave it for about two hours. Then I grill it until it's brown, cut it into squares and eat it with cheese. It's lovely!'

ROSA – AN ARTIST

In restaurants, or at home on Sundays, Italians usually eat four courses[43] for lunch. They begin with the starter, *antipasti*. This may be cold meats and bread, or a salad of tomatoes with fresh mozzarella cheese and basil leaves. Or it may be *bruschetta*, which is grilled[44] bread with fresh tomatoes and garlic[45]. Next is the first course, *primo*. This may be a small plate of pasta, or a rice dish[46] called *risotto*, or a polenta dish. Many Italians eat pasta often, perhaps every day, but they do not eat a big plate of it for a main meal.

The second course, *secondo*, is the meat or fish dish with vegetables and bread. The last course is usually fruit. Sometimes Italians have special desserts and sweets, but not every day. The meal often ends with an espresso coffee and a biscuit, or a piece of dark chocolate.

Drinks

Italians drink a lot of coffee! Espresso is always black, without milk, and is drunk any time of the day. Cappuccino and caffè latte have a lot of milk in them, and are drunk for breakfast. Italians drink water with meals, and some adults enjoy wine. More than two thousand different types of grape[47] are grown in Italy, and wine has been an important part of Italian life since the Ancient Romans. *Aperitivi* is a drink in a bar, with a snack of cold or hot food. This is usually had between 5pm and 8pm.

> Special festivals called Truffle Fairs are at weekends in October and November in Piedmont, Tuscany, Umbria and Marche. The most famous and longest is the Alba Truffle Festival in Piedmont. It is from the middle of October to the middle of November.

Regional foods

The North

Piedmont is a region that grows a lot of rice, and in the north-east Italians eat more rice than pasta. This region is famous for its mushrooms[48]. The most famous one, the white truffle, is often called 'Italy's white gold'. These truffles are very difficult to find so they are very expensive – as much as three thousand euros for one kilogram! Very thin pieces are put on pasta and salads in the very best restaurants round the world.

In Lombardy, the people from Milan are very proud of their *Risotto alla Milanese*, which includes yellow saffron. This is the inside of a small flower called a crocus, and is very expensive. The special risotto rice comes from the Po Valley and Ticino Valley. Unlike other parts of Italy, in this region cooks do not use tomatoes very much. Lombardy is one of the largest cheese-making regions in Italy and this is where gorgonzola cheese comes from.

Gorgonzola cheese

The cuisine of Trentino-Alto Adige includes many Austrian, Hungarian and Slavic dishes with meat and game – wild birds and animals killed for food. Fish and seafood from Lake Garda and the Adriatic Sea are very popular in Veneto. A red salad leaf, *radicchio*, and the coffee dessert *tiramisu* come from this region. Venetians are also famous for their cakes. Friuli-Venezia Giulia is best known for its beef and dairy products. Emilia-Romagna is famous for its balsamic vinegar – a dark liquid made from sweet grapes – and for its Parmigiano-Reggiano cheese. Liguria's famous pesto is made with nuts, basil and olive oil. It is put on pasta or potatoes.

Central Italy

Tuscans enjoy simple, slow-cooked dishes with meat and vegetables. In Umbria, too, people like simple dishes with lots of vegetables. They also eat fish from the River Tiber and a black truffle that grows near Norcia. In Marche, cooks 'stuff' food. In other words[P],they put food inside other food. They make olives stuffed with meat, and chicken or fish stuffed with vegetables. Stuffed pasta, like *ravioli*, comes from central Italy.

Perugia, in Umbria, is famous for its chocolate, and every October there is a chocolate festival.

Abruzzo is famous for its local saffron. Italians in this mountainous region eat a lot of lamb – young sheep – cooked over a very hot flame.

Dishes in Rome and other parts of Lazio use a lot of olive oil, garlic and often anchovies – small fish dried in salt. Meat dishes can include almost every part of the animal, which may surprise some tourists. But almost all tourists love Italian ice cream, *gelato*, as much as Italians do. However, the Sicilians were the first Italians to make it, and people say that they make the best ice cream in the world!

The South

Pizza was first made in Naples, and *Pizza Napoletana* is perhaps the simplest with only tomato, garlic, and basil. Pizzas are eaten all over Italy and the best pizzas are always cooked over a wood-burning fire. In the south, grilled meat, fish and vegetables are simple but very good with a little olive oil and lemon over them.

Puglia makes more olive oil than any other region in Italy and it is famous for its seafood. Calabria grows wonderful oranges and lemons, and their lemon cake is a special dessert. Calabria used to be a poor region and the

Pizza

people needed a way to keep food for the winter months, so they dried or salted food. Sundried tomatoes and anchovies continue to be popular today.

Sicilians like sweets and so family recipes for sweets and biscuits are passed down from mothers to daughters. A dessert from Sicily that is very popular is *cassata*, a cheesecake made with ricotta cheese.

Everywhere in Italy, visitors enjoy the food that Italians have eaten for hundreds and even thousands of years. And what a wonderful place to enjoy it – where there is so much history!

4 A Short History

Etruscan art

The Etruscans

Back in Italy's oldest times, as far back as 700,000 BC, people lived in big groups called tribes. They lived in caves, which are large holes inside mountains. The first group of people that we know something about are the Etruscans. The Etruscans lived mainly between the River Tiber and the River Arno from around the 800s BC. As the Romans grew more powerful, they fought wars with the Etruscans. In 509 BC, the last Etruscan king lost his land to the Romans and the Roman Republic[49] became the most powerful group in the land.

The Roman Republic

After the last Etruscan king lost power, the people chose their government in Rome. Every year they chose two rulers, called consuls. The consuls worked with a group of men, called the Senate. Another group of men, called the Lower Assembly, worked with them but they had less power than the Senate.

The Appian Way was one of the most important Ancient Roman roads. It was built in 312 BC and went from Rome to Brindisi in south-east Italy. Today, visitors to Rome can walk along it and in some places it is even used by cars!

For the first two hundred years of the Republic, Rome's power grew from central Italy to all parts of the Mediterranean world. Later, the Republic ruled in northern Africa, the Iberian Peninsula (now Spain and Portugal), Greece and Gaul (now southern France). From 264 to 146 BC, Rome fought the powerful city of Carthage (now Tunis) in three terrible wars called the Punic Wars. They fought for power in the Mediterranean region.

Too many wars were fought in the time of the Roman Republic. By 49 BC one great soldier knew that he had to change Rome's government.

509 BC	312 BC	264–241 BC	218–201 BC	149–146 BC	49 BC	44 BC
last Etruscan king	Appian Way is built	first Punic War	second Punic War	third Punic War	Julius Caesar becomes the Republic's most powerful man	Augustus becomes the first Roman emperor

The Roman Empire

Historians[50] say that the Roman Republic ended and the Roman Empire began in 49 BC, when soldier Julius Caesar became ruler. But he was not ruler for long because he was killed in 44 BC by Marcus Brutus's men. Then, Octavian (later called Augustus) became the first emperor of Rome. Augustus was very powerful. He had the final decision in government and the army had to follow his orders. In other words, he was a dictator.

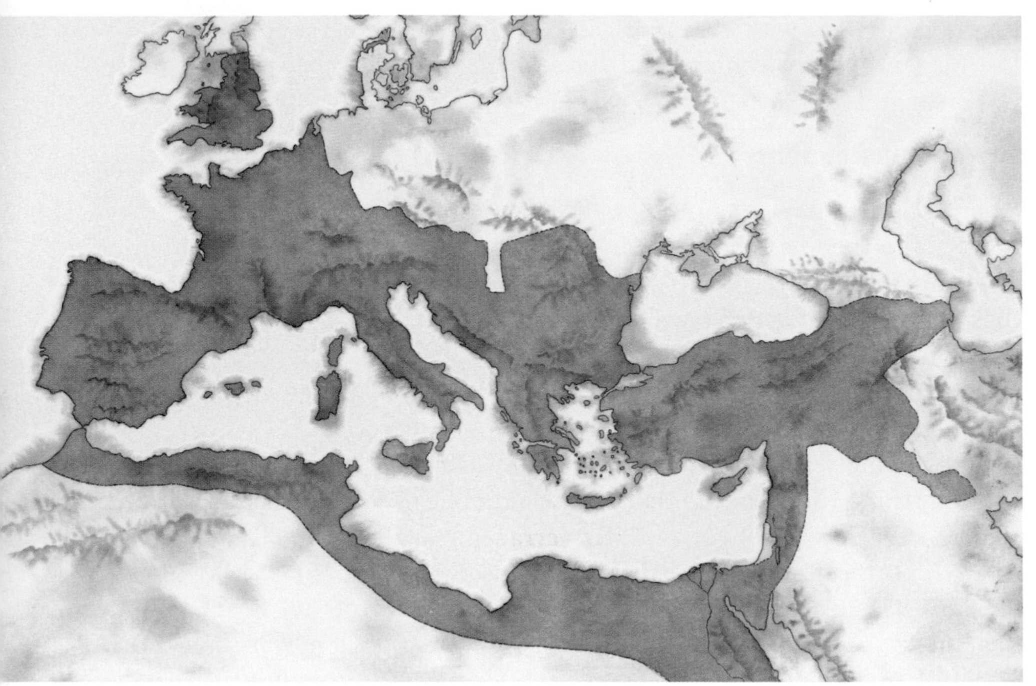

The Roman Empire

Roman cities and towns

By AD 100, the population of Rome was more than 1 million. It had become a very rich city with beautiful buildings and temples. The city had police and fire-fighters. Life in Rome was wonderful for rich people. They had beautiful big homes, the best food, and power.

The Roman army was very well organized. They moved from Italy to most of the rest of the Mediterranean world in the first two centuries AD. In these places the Romans built cities and towns with strong walls around them, good roads, aqueducts and public baths.

i

Emperor Claudius's army of forty thousand soldiers invaded[51] England in AD 43. They fought England's tribes for four years. After this, they ruled the south of the island and later moved north. But Scotland, which is north of England, was never taken by the Romans. In the second century AD, Emperor Hadrian built a large wall, called Hadrian's Wall, in the north of England. This was to keep the Scottish out of England. Hadrian's Wall was about 120 kilometres long and people can visit some of it today.

A Roman city

The Romans believed in many gods. This included gods from the many lands that they invaded. But Christianity grew powerful in the Roman Empire after Constantine I made it the national religion[52] in AD 324. For centuries, popes fought emperors over who was the most powerful ruler. The popes[53] decided to give the rulers of modern-day Germany and France a part to play[P] in Italy. Their king, Charlemagne, was made the Holy Roman Emperor on Christmas Day in the year AD 800.

Language

The Romans made sure that all people in the empire used their language, Latin, in government and law. Over time, Latin divided into other languages. We call these the Romance languages and they include Spanish, Portuguese, French, Italian and Romanian.

OVIDII NASON
HEROÏDES.
EPISTOLA PRIMA.
ARGUMENTUM.
*to Trojano bello ob raptam à Paride Helenam, habitóque à Græc
ventu, invitus cogitur Ulysses ad bellum proficisci: in qua expe
multa adeò & designavit præclarè & gessit, ut excisa tandem Tro
xima illi laus adscriberetur. Peractâ ultione, Trojâque funditus
sâ, victores Græci in patriam redeuntes, spoliis hostium ditati, in
tione læsa Minervæ, variis acti sunt procellis, adeò, ut multis o
pauci post varios errores evaserint. Inter quos Ulysses (ad qu
epistola dirigitur) decem errans annos, peragravit varias orbis
Penelope igitur, ejus uxor, ignara quidem ubi hæreat, valde tame
cita de ejusdem reditu, scribit ei hanc epistolam, quâ cum primis
deat monet, maximè, cùm & Trojâ jam excisâ, aliisque reversis
nullam cunctandi causam habeat.*

Latin

Dividing the empire

By the fourth century, the Roman Empire was so large that it was necessary to divide it into east and west. Rome continued as the capital of the Western Empire. In AD 330, Emperor Constantine I made Constantinople (now Istanbul in Turkey) the capital city of the Eastern Empire. Today, there are about forty modern countries in what was the Roman Empire.

Many reasons are given for the end of the Roman Empire in AD 410. Some of these reasons include:

- The army became too powerful in choosing emperors.
- Emperors such as Caligula and Nero spent too much of the empire's money on big parties.
- Poor people lost their homes and had to live on the streets. The streets of Rome were dangerous because there was a lot of crime.
- The Roman Empire lost power to Germanic invaders, called barbarians.

After the Roman Empire

The fifth to the tenth centuries AD became known as the Dark Ages. In Rome, and most of Europe, culture was destroyed[54]. Learning to read and write was no longer important and no great architecture was built. Invaders from Spain, France and Austria took power away from Italy. Christians lost power in northern Europe, too. Life did not begin to get better in Italy until much later.

Powerful cities

Between the twelfth and fourteenth centuries, cities such as Florence, Milan, Venice, Genoa, Parma, Bologna and Padua grew very powerful. They were known as city-states. In some city-states, rich, important families such as the Medici in Florence and the Visconti and Sforza in Milan had great power. As a result of their fight for power, wars were fought between regions. One of the strongest city-states was Venice because it controlled[55] the Adriatic Sea. But Milan, too, became a strong European power.

> **i** Marco Polo (1254–1324) was born into a rich family of traders[56] from Venice. In 1271, he went with his father and uncle to Asia. There they lived in the lands of the Chinese emperor, Kublai Khan, who sent Marco Polo to many parts of China. When Polo returned to Venice twenty-four years later, his city was at war with Genoa. The Genoese put Polo in prison. There he met the writer Rustichello from Pisa and he told him about his travels. Rustichello wrote a very popular book called *The Travels of Marco Polo*.

A new beginning

From the fourteenth to the sixteenth centuries, well-educated[57] men became interested in Ancient Greek and Roman writers and thinkers. New ideas began to grow. With financial help from the Medici family in Florence, artists, writers, musicians and thinkers brought a new beginning to Italy and to the Western World. This was the start of the Renaissance, which means 'born again'. The historian, writer and political thinker Machiavelli brought fresh, new ideas. But one man who has become known as the true 'Renaissance Man' was Leonardo da Vinci.

Leonardo da Vinci was a painter, sculptor, architect, musician, engineer, inventor[58] and writer and today he is known as 'the father of modern science'.

Italy: a new country

As time passed, the city-states slowly lost power. Much of Italy was controlled by Spain or France by the late sixteenth century. Lombardy, Mantua, Naples and Sardinia were controlled by Austria. By the eighteenth century, the Italian regions were no longer very important in world politics. In 1734, Spain controlled Naples and Sicily. In 1805, Napoleon, emperor of France, made himself the king of Italy, or more exactly the northern half of the country. A year later, he took Naples. Napoleon wanted the city-states to join together so that they could fight his enemies.

This never really happened and by 1814 Napoleon was gone. From 1860 to 1861, four men worked to bring Italy's city-states together. They were Giuseppe Mazzini, a politician, Giuseppe Garibaldi, a politician and soldier, Camillo Benso di Cavour, the prime minister[59] of Piedmont, and the Savoy king Vittorio Emanuele II from Sardinia. Garibaldi's followers fought hard and in March 1861, the fighting ended. Vittorio Emanuele II became the king of Italy and Cavour became Italy's first prime minister.

Cavour

Mussolini and the Second World War

In 1922, Benito Mussolini and his followers, called Fascists, went into Rome and took power. King Vittorio Emanuele III was worried so did not try to stop him. Mussolini made himself '*Il Duce*' – the Leader[60]. He wanted a new Roman Empire so in 1935 he invaded Abyssinia (now Ethiopia). He knew that the war would help stop the Italian people thinking about their country's economic problems. In the Second World War, Mussolini joined with Hitler of Germany. He was killed on 28th April 1945. After the Second World War, Italy borrowed money from the United States of America (USA). At this time, the USA offered money to European countries to rebuild their economies.

The government after the Second World War

In 1946, Italy became a republic again. The Italian government has two groups or houses called the Senate and the Chamber of Deputies. Every seven years, the people choose one person to be president. But the prime minister, who is also chosen by the people, is the person with the real power.

The economy

After the Second World War, many Italians moved from the countryside to the cities. Millions of people moved from the south to the north. In the northern cities Italian companies were making cars, such as Fiat and Lamborghini. They also had some of the world's most famous fashion houses, such as Gucci and Armani. In the 1950s and 60s, Italy became internationally famous for design and fashion. From the 1950s to the 1970s, the country became economically powerful in the world again. In 1957, Italy put its name to an important document called the Treaty of Rome. This was the beginning of the European Economic Community, now the European Union. The 1980s and 90s were more difficult years economically. Then in January 1999, Italy joined the European countries that use the euro.

The euro has made it easier for Europeans to travel to other European countries. As a result, many Europeans go to Italy to visit the wonderful museums and to see some of the world's best art.

5 Art

Trajan's Column in Rome

Italian art has been famous around the world for many centuries. From the art of the Etruscans to the art in modern Italy, we can see how art has changed over time.

Roman art

> After Christianity became the national religion, art became less about war. It became more about how to live a Christian life. Art was not about the great emperors, but about religion.

Much of Classical Roman art told the story of wars that the Romans had fought and won. An example of this is *Trajan's Column* in Rome. The Romans built large stone arches with reliefs[61] of men at war on them. Sculptures were often of powerful emperors sitting on their horses, such as *Marcus Aurelius* in the Campidoglio in Rome. When Hadrian was emperor, he had many beautiful sculptures inside his country house in Tivoli. The Roman mosaic was used in all parts of the Roman Empire, mainly on floors and walls. It was also used in Christian art.

Romanesque and Gothic architecture

> After the Romanesque and before the Renaissance there was Gothic architecture. Milan's cathedral is Italy's best example of Gothic architecture. Work on the cathedral started in 1387.

Architecture was important in Italian art in the thirteenth and fourteenth centuries. This was later called Romanesque architecture. Artists such as painters, sculptors, glass-workers and metal-workers worked with architects on churches and cathedrals. In Rome's Basilica of Santa Maria Maggiore there are also wonderful mosaics and sculptures.

Gothic sculptors

Nicola Pisano, who worked from 1258–84, was an architect and sculptor. His beautiful work can be seen inside Siena Cathedral and in the church building, the baptistery, next to Pisa Cathedral. His son, Giovanni Pisano, was also a great sculptor. His work can be seen in Pisa Cathedral. Another Pisano sculptor, but with no relationship to Nicola, was Andrea Pisano. He worked from 1330-37 on the South Doors of the baptistery next to Florence Cathedral.

Gothic painters

An important painter of the natural human figure[62] in the thirteenth century was Cimabue. Cimabue's *Santa Trinita Madonna* is in the Uffizi in Florence. Another important painter was Giotto di Bondone (1267–1337) from Florence. He also worked in Rome, Padua, Milan and Naples. His

The East Doors of the baptistery next to Florence Cathedral

paintings in a church in Padua told stories in a way that was completely new at the time. Bondone had a feeling for the human figure and for human passion. This makes his paintings special even today.

The Renaissance 1250–1500

Sculptors

The word 'Renaissance', which means 'born again' is not a modern word. It was used in the fifteenth century. This was an exciting time in Italy. There was better government, people were richer and new inventions were changing the world. Renaissance artists wanted to make their sculptures and paintings more natural. They wanted to bring their works to life with humans that had human feelings. Works of art were no longer made mainly for the Catholic Church. Other people had money and power and could buy art. Artists began making paintings and sculptures to put in government buildings, kings' palaces and in the large homes of rich families. Florence was the centre of Renaissance art for much of the fifteenth century. The richest and most powerful family of bankers there was the Medici family. They paid the best artists to make paintings and sculptures for them.

Donatello's *St George*

Lorenzo Ghiberti (1378–1455) is known as the first Renaissance artist. His relief work on the East Doors of the baptistery in Florence shows the change from Gothic to Early Renaissance art. His work showed human figures with human feelings. This was quite new.

Perhaps the most famous sculptor of this time was Donatello (1386–1466). Donatello was Ghiberti's student. His new ideas for relief work can be seen in his life-size figure of *St George* in Florence. The figure looks ready to move. Donatello was a favourite sculptor of the Medici family.

Painters

In the fifteenth century, painting became more important than sculpture or architecture for the first time in the Western World. Painters started to paint their figures and objects using perspective – drawing objects to give a feeling of how deep or far things are. Some of the best painters gave their figures human feelings.

Masaccio (1401–28) worked for another rich family, the Brancacci family of Florence. He was the first artist to make what we now call Renaissance paintings. His figures' faces and bodies tell us much about human feelings. He learnt to paint figures from studying the sculptures of the great Donatello. A good example of his work is *The Tribute Money* (1425–28).

Filippo Lippi (1457–1504) first learnt to paint from his father, also a painter. After his father died, he worked for the famous artist Botticelli. Botticelli had been a student of Lippi's father. Lippi worked with Botticelli on frescoes for Lorenzo de' Medici. He also learnt from Masaccio how to use light in his paintings. Lippi's work later became very important to a group of painters in the nineteenth century, called the Pre-Raphaelites.

The Medici family had their favourite artists and they spent a lot of money on paintings and sculptures to put in their large houses. Art historians think that Botticelli's *Primavera* (about 1478) and *Birth of Venus* (about 1483) were probably painted for the Medici family. Botticelli took the ideas for these paintings from two well-known myths. His idea for the painting *Primavera* came from the Greek goddess Chloris. Chloris became the Roman goddess of flowers and spring, and was called Flora. She was taken from her home by Zephyr, the god of the west wind, and she later married him. By 1500, people were less interested in Botticelli's paintings and his work did not become popular again until the nineteenth century.

One of the first Renaissance artists to sign a painting – to write his name on his painting – was Giovanni Bellini (1430–1516). Bellini came from a family of Venetian artists, and one of his pupils was the artist Titian.

Primavera: In this painting the wind-god Zephyr runs after Chloris. As he touches her, she is changed into Flora. In the centre of the painting is Venus, the goddess of love.
Birth of Venus: In this painting we see Venus, who was born from the sea. In the myth, she was blown by the west wind to the coast of Cyprus.

High Renaissance 1500–60

Some of the world's greatest works of art come from the Italian High Renaissance. The four most well-known artists were Leonardo da Vinci, Michelangelo, Raphael and Titian.

Leonardo da Vinci (1452–1519)

Leonardo's paintings *Last Supper* and *Mona Lisa* were the first paintings to look quite natural. Many art historians say that Leonardo's *Mona Lisa* was the first modern portrait[63]. Before he painted, Leonardo spent many hours studying the human figure, planning and drawing. He also cut open dead bodies to study the different parts. He wanted to know exactly how the human body looked. When other artists saw his work, they knew that he was a genius[64].

Michelangelo Buonarroti (1475–1564)

Another genius was Michelangelo. In 1496, Michelangelo left Florence and went to Rome. He understood the human figure better than most other artists. He also taught himself by cutting open dead bodies and studying the different parts. His sculpture for the Vatican called *Pietà*, made him famous at the age of twenty-four. In 1505, the pope asked him to make sculptures for his mausoleum – the place where a dead body is put. Later, he asked him to paint the Sistine Chapel. After Michelangelo finished the beautiful fresco in the Sistine Chapel, he returned to working on sculptures. He always said that he was a sculptor first and a painter second. Michelangelo and da Vinci each wanted to be the best artist of their time, but we can now see that each one was a genius.

Raffaello Sanzio (1483–1520)

Better known in English as Raphael, this painter went from Perugia to Florence in 1504. Here he saw works by Leonardo and Michelangelo. He learnt a lot from them, but his own genius was to result in many beautiful paintings of *Madonnas*. These are paintings of the mother of Jesus Christ. Raphael became famous and by 1508 was painting frescoes in the Vatican. His portraits *Portrait of a Man* and *Lady with a Unicorn* are in the Borghese Gallery in Rome. Unfortunately Raphael died very suddenly at the age of thirty-seven. One of his greatest paintings, *The Transfiguration*, was left unfinished.

Tiziano Vecellio (died in 1576)

Another genius, who is called Titian in English, painted his famous *Assumption of the Virgin* in 1516–18. He then painted myths between 1518 and 1523. After he painted portraits of the Holy Roman Emperor Charles V, aristocrats[65] and other rich people all wanted to have their portrait done by the great Titian. Titian returned to painting myths in his old age, such as *Diana and Actaeon* (1558).

Baroque 17th and 18th Centuries

By the end of the sixteenth century, a new kind of artist started creating Baroque paintings. His name was Caravaggio.

Caravaggio's *Cardsharps*

Michelangelo da Caravaggio (1571–1610)

Caravaggio used bright colours and strong light. His paintings gave a fresh look at ways to include Lombard, Venetian, Tuscan and Flemish ideas. Caravaggio painted people enjoying life, such as *The Musicians*. He also made religious paintings such as *Madonna dei Pellegrini*, which told a story in a down-to-earth[66] way.

Giovanni Antonio Canal (1697–1768)

This artist is known as Canaletto today. He painted landscapes[67] of Venice, a city that had become a tourist centre for rich people. Visitors from England bought many of his paintings, and Canaletto moved to London in 1746. He made many paintings of London, including *Westminster Bridge*. But the English became bored with his paintings and he returned to Venice in 1755.

By the eighteenth century, rich people were putting paintings on the walls in their city houses. They enjoyed paintings of people having a good time by the popular artists Pietro Longhi and Giandomenico Tiepolo.

Art was important and it was changing. By the twentieth century people were looking to the future. This brought on a new kind of art called Futurism. Futurist paintings were about modern life and machines, and the artists used bright colours.

Important works of art, including architecture, sculpture and paintings can be found across Italy. People from countries round the world know the names of many of these works and the artists who made them. And as important as Italian art is Italian literature[68].

6 Literature

A mosaic of Virgil

The works of Italy's best writers are national treasures. Many of these works are world treasures. Ancient Roman myths are an important part of Western culture even today. We see the names of mythological gods and goddesses in names of shops and restaurants, in titles of modern books, and we hear their names in modern songs. And the myths are repeated in many different ways in today's literature.

A golden age of Latin

Prose[69] writers

Latin was the language of Ancient Rome. Some of the most well-known prose writers of that time were rulers, politicians, poets and historians. The powerful ruler Julius Caesar (100–44 BC) wrote about the wars that he and the Roman army won in *The Conquest of Gaul* and *The Civil War*. Caesar's works are important even today. Another politician at the time of Caesar was Cicero (106–43 BC). Cicero is said to be the greatest public speaker in the history of the world. His written works include *On the Republic* and *On the Laws*.

The Roman historian Titus Livius Patavinus, known as Livy in English, (59 BC–AD 17) wrote *History of Rome*. In it he explained the complete history of Rome from its beginning, to the end of emperor Augustus's rule. Later (about AD 45–120), a Greek and Roman historian called Plutarch wrote about the lives of a number of famous people in his book *The Parallel Lives*.

Poets

Many of the poets from Ancient Rome continue to be read today. Catullus (about 84–54 BC), a Latin poet, wrote poems that were important to later poets such as Ovid, Horace and Virgil. His poems are still read in schools today. Ovid (43 BC–AD 17) wrote poems about love. His most famous poem, written in fifteen books, was *Metamorphoses*. It is one of the most important works of classical mythology. Ovid was very popular, but he was sent away from Rome by Augustus and never returned. Historians have never learnt exactly why he was sent away. Ovid himself wrote that it was because of 'a poem and a mistake'.

Another important poet in the golden age of Rome, under Augustus, was Horace (65–8 BC). European poets have learnt much of what they know from his poetry. A poet who liked to mix myths and Roman history was Virgil (70–19 BC). He wrote the poem *The Aeneid*, which told the story of Aeneas and the beginning of Rome. Unfortunately Virgil died before he finished this poem. Another Roman poet was Juvenal (about AD 55–127). His poetry often made fun of[P] rich people including the emperor Domitian. His book of poems, *Satires*, has taught us a lot about Roman people and their lives.

6

Dante Alighieri

The Renaissance

Poets

There were many important Italian poets from the fourteenth to the sixteenth centuries. One of the most important works of world literature was the poem *The Divine Comedy* written by Dante Alighieri (1265–1321). It was written in the language of Tuscany, which became the Italian language that we know today. Dante is called 'the father of the Italian language'. *The Divine Comedy* is about life after people die. It is a story about Dante's travels through Hell, Purgatory and Heaven – some Christians believe people go to one of these three places after they die. Hell is the worst place, Purgatory is better than Hell and Heaven is the best place to go. In *The Divine Comedy* the Roman poet Virgil takes Dante through Hell and Purgatory. Dante is finally taken through Heaven by his true love Beatrice.

Francesco Petrarca, known in English as Petrarch, fell in love with Laura de Noves in 1327. Petrarch wrote 366 love poems about Laura. These included 317 sonnets – poems with fourteen lines. As a result, it is said that Petrarch made the Italian sonnet popular. In 1341, Petrarch went to Rome. Here he became Poet Laureate – the name for the best poet chosen to write for the king.

'I think everyone should read Boccaccio's *Decameron*. It is a group of ten stories told over ten days by ten storytellers. The storytellers have left Florence because many people are dying from the plague[70]. The plague happened in 1348 and about 100,000 people in Florence died. The storytellers are three aristocrats and seven ladies. They tell stories about how people behaved at that time.'

ANTONIO – A TEACHER FROM BARI

Giovanni Boccaccio (1313–75) began writing his best known work *Decameron* in about 1349. Boccaccio met Petrarch in Florence in 1350 and they became friends. As a result of their conversations, Boccaccio wrote *On the Genealogy of the Gods of the Gentiles*. This is a book about the family relationships of important Ancient Greek and Roman gods. It continued to be an important book on classical mythology for over four hundred years.

Italian actors

Theatre

In the sixteenth century the first professional type of theatre called *Commedia dell'arte* started in Italy. Actors performed[71] in the streets and everyone could enjoy the performance for free. However, the best theatre groups performed inside castles for kings. Everyone enjoyed laughing at people in love, stupid old men and soldiers who thought that they could win every fight. Carlo Goldoni later wrote over 150 comedies. Many later writers of plays, called playwrights, got their ideas from *Commedia dell'arte*, including the sixteenth century English playwright William Shakespeare.

> Some of Shakespeare's plays happen in Italy –
> **Venice:** *The Merchant of Venice* and *Othello*
> **Verona and Milan:** *The Two Gentlemen of Verona*
> **Padua:** *The Taming of the Shrew*
> **Rome:** *Coriolanus*, *Julius Caesar* and *Titus Andronicus*
> **Sicily:** *The Winter's Tale*

Eighteenth to twenty-first century literature

Italian writers have continued to write some of the world's best literature. Giacomo Leopardi was one of Italy's greatest poets. He lived from 1798 to 1837. His work *The Zibaldone* is 2,500 pages of his ideas on life and

Popular novels and other literature

- 1883 – Carlo Collodi wrote one of the world's favourite children's stories *Pinocchio*. It is about a wooden boy whose nose grows every time he lies.
- 1947 – Primo Levi's *If This is a Man* told the true story of the year he was in Auschwitz, Poland from 1944–45.
- 1947 – Carlo Levi's most famous book *Christ Stopped at Eboli* opened the eyes[P] of many Italians to the difficult lives of the very poor people in Basilicata at that time.
- 1957 – *The Leopard* by Giuseppe di Lampedusa is the story of aristocrats in the 1860s, as Italy was ready to become one country.
- 1972 – Italo Calvino's *Invisible Cities* started his long and popular career as a novelist. In this book he invented conversations between Marco Polo and the Chinese ruler Kublai Khan.
- 1980 – Umberto Eco wrote about his passion for the Middle Ages in his historical mystery *The Name of the Rose*.

literature. His very negative way of writing about humans and their world was called Historical Pessimism.

Since 1901, the Nobel Prize for Literature has gone to the person who wrote the best work of that year. The writer can be from any country. Italians won this award in 1906, 1926, 1934, 1959, 1975 and 1997.

In 1921 the Sicilian playwright Luigi Pirandello wrote his most famous play *Six Characters in Search of an Author*. Following that he wrote *Henry IV*. Pirandello wrote forty-three plays. He also wrote novels, poems and short stories. In 1934 he won the Nobel Prize for Literature, an international prize given each year to one of the world's most important writers.

In 1994 Andrea Camilleri wrote *The Shape of Water*, the first of many novels about a detective[72] called Montalbano. Since then his novels have been made into a popular television series called *Inspector Montalbano* in English. This series can be seen on television in many countries including the United Kingdom (UK) and the USA. Camilleri was a well-known film and theatre director[73] before he started writing novels. His books have been published[74] in many other languages.

Italy has given the world some of its greatest works of literature over many centuries. And it has also given the world some of the greatest pieces of music and some of the world's best films.

7 Music and Film

La Scala in Milan

Italy is famous around the world for its wonderful operas and beautiful classical music. Italians write and perform other types of music, too, including jazz and pop. There are lots of music festivals in Italy. One of the oldest musical festivals in Europe, which began in 1937, is the Holy Music Festival in Perugia. People who love jazz enjoy the Umbria Jazz Festival. The San Remo Festival of popular music includes pop, rock, folk and other types of modern music. One very popular pop singer today is Eros Ramazzotti, who sings in Italian and Spanish. Another internationally famous pop and rock singer is Zucchero. He has sold over forty million CDs round the world. But Italians are most proud of introducing opera to the rest of the world.

Opera

Jacopo Peri wrote the first opera at the beginning of the seventeenth century for the wedding of Henry IV of France and Marie de' Medici in Florence. Opera includes music, words and drama[75], and quickly became very popular. It has continued to be popular for over four hundred years. Operas are performed in opera houses in most large Italian cities and towns, and across the world today. The San Carlo Theatre in Naples is Europe's oldest opera house. But almost everyone agrees that the greatest opera house in Italy is the beautiful La Scala in Milan.

Composers

Claudio Monteverdi (1567–1643) composed operas to include an orchestra and singers in costumes[76]. He introduced more drama in his operas, too. Italian opera groups travelled to other European cities and composers such as Handel and Mozart were soon writing operas too.

Popular operas

In the nineteenth century, Romantic opera composer Gioacchino Rossini wrote operas which are still performed today, such as *The Barber of Seville*. One of the greatest composers of all time, Giuseppe Verdi, tried new kinds of music and drama in his operas. His 1893 opera, *Falstaff*, was different from other operas because his singers used the same words as ordinary people at that time. In the twentieth century, Giacomo Puccini wrote the very popular operas *La Bohème*, *Turandot, Tosca* and *Madame Butterfly*.

Opera singers

Italian continued to be the language of opera for a long time. But today operas are sung in other languages, such as German, French and English. The songs are called 'arias'. One of Italy's many great tenors[77] was Enrico Caruso, who came from a poor family in Naples. He became internationally famous at the beginning of the twentieth century.

One of today's internationally famous female opera singers is Cecilia Bartoli. She was born in Rome in 1966 and her career began in 1987 in *The Barber of Seville*. She has won awards in many counties including Italy, the USA, the UK, Germany and France. In 2013 she won her tenth ECHO Classics Award.

Actors perform on stage during rehearsals of *La Bohème* opera at La Fenice Theatre in Venice

The very famous Luciano Pavarotti

One of Italy's much-loved tenors, Luciano Pavarotti, was born in Modena, Italy in 1935. He started studying music seriously when he was nineteen years old. About eleven years later, he performed for the first time at Milan's La Scala in *La Bohème.* At the 2006 Winter Olympics in Turin, Pavarotti performed for the last time. Pavarotti made opera really popular because many of his concerts were on television. It was a sad day for opera fans when he died in 2007.

In the Roman Baths of Caracalla in Rome, the three great opera singers Luciano Pavarotti, Placido Domingo and Jose Carreras performed their first 'Three Tenors Concert' in 1990. The CD of that concert is the best-selling CD of classical music of all time.

'I love opera and I was very excited when I saw Luciano Pavarotti perform in London's Hyde Park on 30th July 1991. I was with about 100,000 people and we stood in the rain to listen to him. Britain's Prince Charles and Princess Diana met him after the concert. In the newspapers the next day, there was a photo of the prince and princess. They were very wet, next to the dry and happy Pavarotti!'

ANGELA – AN ACTRESS

Classical music

> The first violins were made in the 1530s in Cremona in Lombardy. Antonio Stradivari (1644–1737) cut down trees in the Dolomite Mountains to make his Stradivarius violins. He made hundreds of violins in his lifetime. About four hundred of these are in the world today. They cost millions of euros!

Many Italian composers of classical music are internationally known. These include Cavalieri, Scarlatti, Boccherini and Paganini. Another of Italy's much loved classical composers is Antonio Vivaldi. This Baroque composer, born in Venice in 1678, wrote the very popular *Four Seasons*. He is mainly known for his violin concertos.

Andrea Bocelli is one of Italy's most famous tenors today. He was born in Tuscany in 1958 and has sold up to 65 million CDs. These include arias from *La Bohème* and *Tosca*. Bocelli is also a songwriter, musician and pop singer. He is now a rich and famous man, but his money can never buy the thing he lost at the age of twelve. He is **blind**, which means he cannot see. One day when he was playing football, he was hit on the head. That accident left him blind. But that does not stop him from performing on television and all round the world.

Film

Before the Second World War, Mussolini's government built a new town for making films called Cinecittà, It had everything that was necessary for film-making and has continued to be used by directors since then. Famous directors including Roberto Rossellini and Federico Fellini made films there. Rossellini made many important films including *Rome Open City* (1945), *Paisa* (1946) and *Germany Year Zero* (1948). Fellini's films taught later directors perhaps more about film-making than any other director. He made great films like *La Strada* (1954) *La Dolce Vita* (1960) and *Spirits of the Dead* (1969).

> Monica Bellucci is a very popular Italian actress today. She was born in Umbria in 1964. She became one of Italy's most famous fashion models. In 1989 she decided to study to become an actress. She has made many popular films including *The Matrix Reloaded* (2003), and *The Sorcerer's Apprentice* (2010). She has won several awards for best actress.

In 1960, the beautiful Italian actress Sophia Loren won an important film prize in America, the Academy Award for Best Actress. This was for her part in Vittorio De Sica's film *Two Women*. She was the first actress to win this award for a film made outside the USA.

After the Second World War, films were made in colour, mainly comedies and costume dramas. Films about America's Wild West became popular, and they were cheaper to make in Italy than in the USA. Italian directors began to make 'Spaghetti Westerns', as they were called, including Sergio Leone's *The Good, The Bad and The Ugly* with the American actor Clint Eastwood.

In the 1980s a lot of comedy films were made in Italy that were not popular internationally. But Italian cinema got much more popular in the late 1980s and in the 1990s. Giuseppe Tornatore's film *Cinema Paradiso* (1988) won an Academy Award for the best film made outside the USA. Gabriele Salvatores's film *Mediterraneo* (1991) won the same award. And Roberto Benigni's film *Life is Beautiful* (1997) won three Academy Awards.

In the twenty-first century, Italian directors have continued to make very popular films. In 2001, Nanni Moretti won the Palme d'Or award at the Cannes Film Festival in France for *The Son's Room*. In 2008, Matteo Garrone won the Grand Prix award at the same festival for his film *Gomorra*.

The Venice Film Festival, which began in 1932, is Italy's most important film festival. It gives awards for best film, best director and best actor and actress. Turin also has an important film festival, and the National Museum of Cinema is one of Turin's very popular museums.

Italy has given a lot to the world of music and to the world of film. But the whole world would be a very different place today if Italian explorers[78] had not sailed to new lands across the Atlantic Ocean. Italian inventors and scientists have made great changes to the world, too. Who were these people and how has their work changed the lives of people everywhere?

8 Explorers, Inventors and Scientists

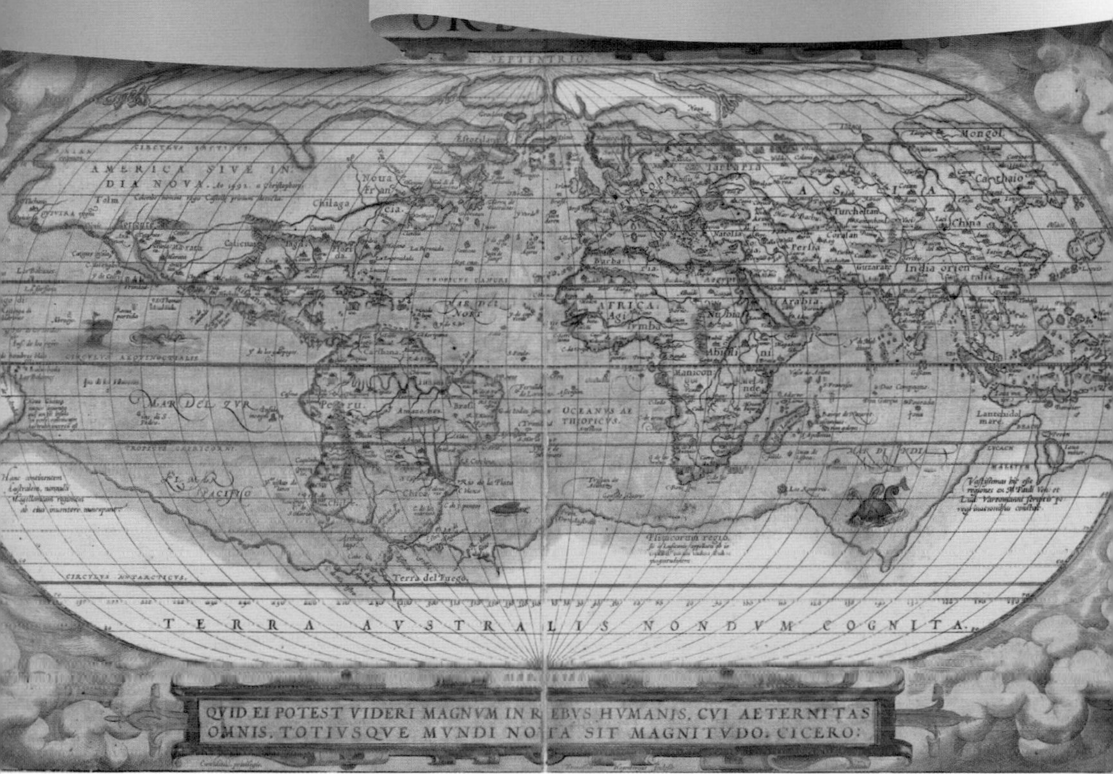

An early world map

Italian explorers are not great in number but the explorers who went to North America are some of the world's most important explorers. Their names are well-known today. Countries, cities and bridges are named after them.

Explorers

In the fifteenth and sixteenth centuries, Italian explorers sailed far away from Europe looking for a route across the sea to China. Kings and explorers knew about Marco Polo's travels in the thirteenth century, and about the wonderful treasures that he found in China and India. But Marco Polo had travelled by land, which was slow. A sea route to the East would take people there much more quickly.

Christopher Columbus (1451–1506)

In 1492, Columbus, who was from Genoa, sailed west looking for a route to the East. To many people it seemed a crazy idea, but he was sure that he was right. King Ferdinand and Queen Isabella of Spain agreed to pay for his voyage[79] so he sailed with the Spanish flag. When Columbus reached land, he was sure that he was in east India. He called the people 'Indians'. But Columbus was not in east India. He was in the Caribbean[80]. For centuries history books have called him the great explorer who discovered[81] America. But now we know that he never once put his foot on land there. The name 'America' probably comes from the Italian explorer Amerigo Vespucci.

Amerigo Vespucci (1454–1512)

Vespucci was a well-educated sailor, explorer and trader from Florence. He was invited by King Manuel I of Portugal to join a Portuguese voyage in 1501. They went to the lands that were discovered by Columbus. They explored lands on the north-eastern coast of South America. Vespucci wrote letters to a friend about what he found there, and those letters were published. Readers were excited about his stories and Vespucci became famous. But not everyone liked Vespucci because he did not agree with the more famous Columbus. Vespucci believed that Columbus's discovery was not in Asia. He believed that it was a 'New World'. At that time it was a big surprise to everyone. A German map-maker was responsible for naming the New World after Amerigo. As more explorers went to America, more water routes, like rivers and lakes, were found. Another explorer was Giovanni da Verrazano.

Giovanni da Verrazano (about 1485–1528)

America's biggest city, New York, has a bridge called the Verrazano Narrows Bridge. It was named after the Italian explorer who sailed for the French king Francis I in 1523. Verrazano explored the Atlantic coast between South Carolina in the USA and Newfoundland, including New York Bay, looking for a route to the Pacific Ocean. He died in 1528 on his third trip to North America.

These and other explorers drew maps that changed the way people understood the world. It became a bigger place with water routes that brought trade to more countries. Trade gave people new ideas, too. It was a time of many new and wonderful inventions.

Inventors and scientists

Leonardo da Vinci (1452–1519)

Leonardo da Vinci was not only a great painter but he was also a very important scientist and inventor. He spent more time working on his ideas in science and technology than on painting. Many of his ideas needed technology that did not exist at that time. He was interested in flight and designed flying machines. He drew the first design for a helicopter. Four centuries later, the first helicopter was flown! He was also the first man to design a parachute, but it too was not made at that time.

It was more than two hundred years later, in 1783, when the parachute was made by the Frenchman Sebastien Lenormand. When Leonardo's design was tested in 2000, it surprised many people because it worked very well. He designed war machines, water machines and many other machines. Leonardo da Vinci was a true Renaissance man. He never went to university but he studied almost everything.

A helicopter and a parachute

Leonardo da Vinci designed a bridge for the ruler of the Ottoman Empire in 1502 to go across the Bosporus. But his design was too difficult for builders of that time so it was never built. However, five hundred years later his design was used, in 2001, for a bridge in Norway. It is now a footbridge over European route E18!

8

Galileo Galilei (1564–1642)

Galileo Galilei

After years of exploring new lands, some Italian explorers reached for the stars[P]. Galileo Galilei was one of them, and he is now called 'the father of modern physics'. Galileo was born in Pisa. Here he studied medicine and later mathematics at the famous University of Pisa. Galileo taught mathematics there and later at the University of Padua. He also taught astronomy, the study of the sun, moon and stars.

Galileo designed and made changes to the telescope, which we use today for looking at the stars. He argued that Aristotle had been wrong about the sun travelling around the Earth. Galileo believed that the Earth travelled around the sun. He published his ideas in *Dialogue Concerning the Two Chief World Systems*. But the Catholic Church believed Aristotle's idea that the Earth was at the centre of everything. As a result of his published ideas, Galileo was found guilty of heresy[82]. That happened on 22nd June 1633. He was not put in prison, but he had to stay inside his house for the rest of his life. He published about twelve main written works in his life including *The Starry Messenger*.

Other inventors

Bartolomeo Cristofori di Francesco (1655–1731) from Padua invented the piano around 1709.

Other famous Italian inventors include Guglielmo Marconi (1874–1937) and Maria Montessori (1870–1952). Marconi invented a new way to send messages. In 1897 he opened the Wireless Telegraph Company in London and people began sending messages round the world.

Maria Montessori, a doctor and teacher, invented a new way to teach children. She believed that not all children learn things at the same time.

Some children learn quickly and others slowly, but they can all learn in their own time. Her educational ideas became very popular, and Montessori schools opened round the world.

'My parents sent me to a Montessori school. It was really good for me. Some very famous people went to Montessori schools and became inventors, including Larry Page and Sergey Brin who started Google. I want to own my own business someday, too!'

GIUSEPPE – A STUDENT

Scientists

Some inventors were scientists, other inventors were not. There are many famous Italian scientists, and their work has changed the way people live. Luigi Galvani (1737–98) from Bologna was a physicist and doctor. His study of the human body resulted in neuroscience – the science of the nervous system[83]. Enrico Fermi (1901–54) was born in Rome and later became an American. He is one of the most important scientists of the twentieth century for his work on the first nuclear reactor[84]. He received the Nobel Prize for Physics in 1938.

All of these Italians have made the world a better place to live. Thanks to them and other people like them, people today live longer and more active lives. Some of the world's most active people are sportsmen and sportswomen. Many of Italy's favourite sports and sports people are famous round the world.

9 Sport

The Juventus football team is from Turin

Most Italians love sport and the most popular sport is football, or *calcio* in Italian. Car racing is also very popular and probably everyone knows the name Ferrari. The country's coast, lakes, rivers and mountains give people lots of choice of water sports and mountain sports. But football is the sport that *everyone* loves to watch and play.

Football

Italy's national team has won the World Cup four times: in 1934, 1938, 1982 and 2006.

Football is a national passion in Italy. The Italian national team is known as *Gli Azzurri*. It plays in UEFA (Union of European Football Associations) and is one of the best teams in the world. The name comes from the colour azure, the blue colour of the team's shirts.

Italy's greatest footballer of all time was perhaps Giuseppe Meazza, born in Milan in 1910. He began playing for the national team in 1930 and continued there until 1939. He was a main player when Italy won the World Cup in 1934 and again in 1938. Meazza became famous for his thirty-three international goals, which is the second highest number in the history of Italian football. He also played for A.C. Milan, Juventus, Varese and Atalanta and later was the manager[85] of a number of teams, including Internazionale. The Internazionale stadium in Milan is named after him.

Turin's team, Juventus, takes its name from the ancient Roman goddess of young men.

The twenty best football teams in the country belong to Serie A, Italy's most important professional football league[86]. By 2013 Turin's team, Juventus, had won Serie A twenty-nine times. Internazionale and A.C. Milan had each won eighteen times.

Juventus Stadium

Today football is big business and teams need to make money from fans. In newly built stadiums there are museums, shops and restaurants. Here fans can spend money and enjoy themselves. Some of Italy's football stadiums are old and need to become more modern. Turin built a new stadium for Juventus with forty-one thousand seats. This opened for the 2011–12 football season. It cost about 100 million euros! Before that, the last stadium built in Italy was in 1990 for the World Cup. Thousands of football fans enjoy watching their teams play in large stadiums like Olympic Stadium in Rome, and Giuseppe Meazza Stadium in Milan.

Many football fans enjoy visiting the National Football Museum in Coverciano in Tuscany, which is where the national teams prepare for the football season. There, fans can look at balls, shoes, clothes and prizes from some of the country's greatest footballers.

Car racing

Italian car designers have made some of the world's fastest racing cars. Some go as fast as 350 kilometres an hour! Winning the Formula One World Championship[87] is the dream of every racing car driver. Formula One, or F1, races are on circuits[88] in countries all over the world, but only one driver and one car-maker can win. Ferrari has won more F1 races than any other car-maker.

A Ferrari F1 racing car

Enzo Ferrari started making racing cars in 1929 at a factory near Bologna. He was not interested in making cars for ordinary drivers. But in 1947 the factory started making ordinary cars so that they could make money to build more racing cars. The company's team is the oldest F1 team that is racing today. Famous drivers like Juan Manuel Fangio, Niki Lauda and Michael Schumacher have all won championships for Ferrari. The Ferrari Museum near the factory gives fans lots of information about the team's history. There is also a cinema for watching great races. Near the factory is the Fiorano racing circuit. This was built in 1972 for fans to see how well they can drive a Ferrari!

Car racing fans have their favourite drivers but one of the best young drivers is Sebastian Vettel. Vettel was born in Germany on 3rd July 1987. At the age of seventeen, he won eighteen out of twenty races in the German Formula BMW championship. He was the first to do that. His first F1 race was in the 2007 US Grand Prix at Indianapolis. He finished in eighth place. He is the youngest person to win Formula One four times in a row[P] *in the sixty-one years of the sport's history. He won his first F1 Championship in 2010 at the age of twenty-three and continued to win in 2011, 2012 and 2013! What does he hope to do in future? Drive for Ferrari, of course!*

Cycling

Italians have won more world cycling championships than almost any other country. Only Belgium has won more.

Cycling is another sport for people who enjoy racing. Cycling is a very popular sport in Italy and every year towards the end of May the *Giro d'Italia* race starts. The route changes every year but the riders always travel through the Alps, including the Dolomites. The race takes around twenty-three days! The first rider to win five times was Alfredo Binda in the 1920s and 30s. In 1950, the race had its first winner who was not an Italian. He was Hugo Koblet from Switzerland.

Cycling is a lovely sport in spring, summer and autumn. But when the snow starts to fall, it is time to go to the mountains for some fun winter sports.

9

Winter sports

Italians enjoy winter sports like skiing, ice skating, bobsleigh and luge.

Bobsleigh

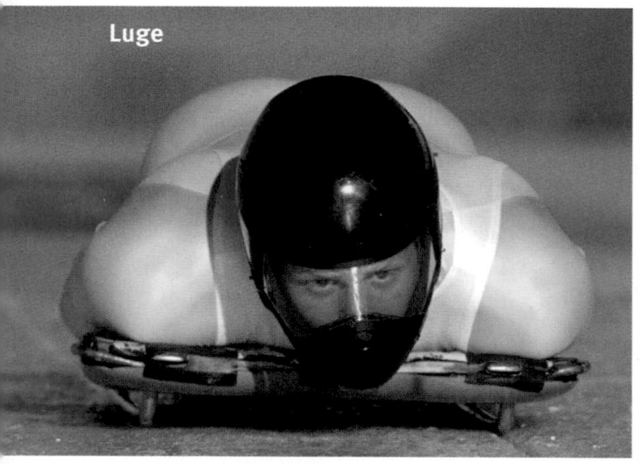

Luge

Ice skating

Skiing

One of the world's best lugers is Armin Zöggler from Merano in South Tyrol. He won the Luge World Cup six years in a row from 2006 to 2011. One of Italy's best skiers is Alberto Tomba, who won Olympic gold medals[89] in 1988 and 1992, and silver medals in 1992 and 1994. But winter sports are not only for professionals. Many Italian families go to the mountains in winter to enjoy winter sports.

Other popular sports

Basketball was made popular in Italy by American soldiers in the Second World War. Today, it is a very popular sport and the Italian league is often said to be one of the best leagues in the world together with the USA, Spain, Greece and Argentina.

> i
>
> Italy sent 282 men and women to the 2012 Olympics in London and they came back home with eight gold medals, nine silver medals and eleven bronze medals. The Italians did very well in many sports including fencing[90], water polo[91] and gymnastics[92].

Water sports like swimming, sailing, boating and water skiing are very popular in Italy. Water polo is a popular water sport. The Italian water polo team won the silver medal at the London Olympics in 2012.

Fencing has been a popular sport in Italy for a long time. Italians won seven fencing medals in the London 2012 Olympics. One of the winners was Valentina Vezzali, who has won six Olympic gold medals. She has also won fourteen gold medals at the World Fencing Championships.

Italians are doing very well in gymnastics. The Italian team won first place in the 2010 Gymnastics Championship in Moscow and won bronze medals in the 2012 London Olympics.

Sport is an important part of life in Italy. In future, Italy hopes to win even more medals, more championships and most importantly the World Cup! But there is more to the future than football. What else can the world expect from Italy in the future?

10 Looking Forward

Future technology

The year 2013 was 'The Year of Italian Culture' in the USA. There were over two hundred events[93] in more than fifty American cities, including San Francisco, Boston and New York. It was organized by the Italian Ministry of Foreign Affairs[94] and the Italian Embassy[95] in Washington, D.C. A large number of Italians went to the USA to promote[96] Italy's culture and cuisine, design and fashion, and science and technology.

Cuisine

Americans love Italian food. One popular food from Italy is Nutella made by Ferrero. Chocolate and nuts are mixed together to put on bread. The USA spends $240.4 million on Nutella each year! But Italy does not sell only its food and drink to the rest of the world. It also sells the machines to make these foods and drinks. Italy is a world leader in food technology machines and it sells over ninety per cent of them abroad each year. Italy makes and sells espresso coffee machines, ice cream machines, fridges, machines for cutting meat and for making bread and pasta. Italian food seems to be getting more and more popular around the world so they will be selling a lot more machines, too!

Design and science

In The Year of Italian Culture, Italian designers and scientists arrived in the USA to promote new inventions in technology and new ways forward in medicine. They wanted Americans to see that Italians are coming up with[P] some very exciting robots[97]. At one event, visitors saw a robot that can go to people's houses to do their recycling. The robot makes the decisions about what to put in each recycling box. It then takes the recycling away. At another event, scientists introduced clothes made of a new kind of cloth. The cloth cleans itself using sunlight! At another event, Italian scientists explained how they are making new bones[98] for the human body. The bones are made of wood, and this works better than plastic. For a long time Italians have been world leaders in inventing new things. Today Italian designers and inventors are coming up with interesting and exciting ways to change our future.

Italians have been famous car-makers for a long time. At the 2013 Geneva Car Show, visitors loved Ferrari's new car called La Ferrari. But they needed to be rich to buy it. Not many visitors could buy Lamborghini's new car, Veneno, either. At that time, they were planning to make only three of these cars, and sell them for US$4 million each! The company is proud of its cars and proud of its country! They were planning to paint the three cars the three colours of Italy's flag: one red, one white and one green. Another Italian company, called Energica, is making an exciting new superbike. This will be sold first in the USA in 2015 for $25,000. People who love cars, love Italian cars because they are special. They are the cars of people's dreams.

A Lamborghini Aventador LP700-4 car is on diplay during the 11th China (Guanzhou) International Automobile exhibition at China Import and Export Fair Complex

But some people's dreams are sky-high! The Italian company Tecnam is the world's number one maker of very light sport aeroplanes. The company, which is near Naples, was started by two brothers in 1948. The company makes about three hundred light sport aeroplanes every year. Each one costs between 70,000 and 300,000 euros. They are sold all over the world to flight schools and to private buyers.

In design and fashion, more exciting things are coming from Italy. The company Italdesign Giugiaro near Turin is best known for car design, but it also makes beautifully designed furniture. Their lamps, tables, beds and designs for bathrooms and kitchens are interesting and very popular. From the region of Marche, Italy's shoe-making region, some of the world's most beautiful shoes and bags are made. Some of the most popular designers are Valentino Garavani, Gianvito Rossi and Sergio Rossi.

Italian designers know how to keep rich people happy! Famous actresses and singers like Jennifer Lopez, Penélope Cruz and Beyoncé like to wear dresses made by Versace. Famous people also seem to like Gucci bags and Ferragamo shoes. On the Italian Riviera, rich people must protect their eyes – with sunglasses made by Dolce and Gabbana, Gucci and Miu Miu.

'My favourite designer is Versace. This is a private company that is owned by the Versace family. I think we will see a lot of new and wonderful designs from them for a long time. When Gianni Versace was killed in Miami, Florida in 1997, his sister Donatella and his brother Santo kept the company going[P]. Gianni's young niece, Allegra, now owns fifty per cent of the $2 billion business!'

ANNA – A BUSINESSWOMAN

Some of Italy's new young designers say that the government does not understand how important fashion is to the economy. They are worried about Italy's future in the world of fashion. But other young designers do not agree. Some of the best young designers in Italy today are Massimo Giorgetti, Andrea Pompilio and Andrea Incontri. They are names to look for in the future.

Family

In 2013 a document on birth rates said that out of 224 countries, Italy was number 203. In 2012 the number of births was 12,000 fewer than in 2011.

The family has always been the centre of Italian life. But some people are worried that this is changing. Italians are having fewer and fewer children. Italy now has one of the lowest birth rates[99] in Europe.

The number of years that Italians are expected to live is eighty-two. In 2013, twenty per cent of Italians were over the age of sixty-five. The government is worried about what this means for the future. Some people say that when the Italian economy gets better, more people will have children. But will they?

Italy spends a lot of money on hospitals and medicine. More babies have a future in Italy than in some of the world's most powerful countries. Fewer babies die in Italy than in most other countries in the world. For every one thousand babies under the age of one year only 3.3 die in Italy. In the UK it is 4.5 babies, and in the USA it is 5.9.

Italy not only spends a lot of money on hospitals and medicine, it also spends a lot of money on transport.

'I'm from Palermo in Sicily but I'm studying in Milan. I'm studying design and technology. I want to design cleaner and safer cars. A lot is happening in Italy today in new transport designs. Here in Milan, we are working on ways to take cars off the roads. I believe that people will share electric cars and motorcycles in future. That will take a lot of cars off the roads, and will be a much cleaner way to travel. I'm really excited about my future career!'

ADRIANA – A STUDENT

Transport

Italy has very fast trains, called high-speed trains, to all of the country's largest cities. The national train company, Trenitalia, has trains that can go over 300 kilometres an hour. The train from Milan to Venice takes just over two hours. Future plans are for a high-speed train across the Alps from Turin to Lyon, France. This will be very good for Turin and for the country. But some people are angry about these plans because the train will go through the beautiful Susa Valley in Piedmont. They say that it will destroy the environment. High-speed trains are the way of the future, but it is very important to protect nature.

Of course, no one can know what the future will bring. But we can be quite sure that Italy will continue to be one of the greatest countries in the world. There are not many, if any, countries that have had more great explorers, inventors, designers, scientists, artists and writers than Italy. It is a country that we look up to[P] and we can expect much more to come from the country and its people.

Points for Understanding

1

1 Where can you find ...

a the Dolomite Mountains?

b Lake Garda?

c the Po Valley?

d the Central Apennines?

e the Adriatic Sea?

2 Where are some of Italy's most beautiful beaches?

3 Which volcano is the highest active volcano in Europe?

4 Where does the word 'volcano' come from?

5 Which park is the largest in the Alps?

6 When was the earthquake in Italy that killed 72,000 people?

2

1 Which river does Rome sit on?

2 Which Roman god is there a sculpture of at the Trevi Fountain in Rome and what is he doing?

3 Where was the centre of politics and law in Ancient Rome?

4 When and where were the first gladiator games?

5 What is the name of Florence's oldest bridge and what river does it go across?

6 What is Italy's second largest city and why is it important?

3

1 Why did Carlo Petrini start the Slow Food Movement?
2 Where in Italy do people eat more polenta than pasta?
3 Which region is famous for truffles and other mushrooms?
4 Which region does not use tomatoes very much in their dishes?
5 Which region makes more olive oil than any other region?
6 How are the best pizzas cooked?

4

1 Who were the first people in Italy that we know something about?
2 Who did the Romans fight between 264 and 146 BC and what were the wars called?
3 Where is Hadrian's Wall and why was it built?
4 What was the population of Rome in AD 100?
5 When and why was the Roman Empire divided into east and west?
6 Which powerful city-state controlled the Adriatic Sea between the twelfth and fourteenth centuries?

5

1 Where did Romans mainly use mosaics?
2 What did Renaissance artists want to do?
3 Which Botticelli painting tells the story of the Roman Goddess Flora?
4 What painting do art historians say is the first modern portrait?
5 Did Michelangelo prefer to paint or to make sculptures?
6 Who did Titian paint portraits of?
7 What did Canaletto paint?

6

1 What did Catullus, Ovid and Horace write?

2 Who is called 'the father of the Italian language' and what did he write?

3 Who became Poet Laureate in 1341?

4 How many stories are in Boccaccio's *Decameron* and who are the storytellers?

5 Which modern writer wrote about his passion for the Middle Ages?

7

1 What did Monteverdi's operas include?

2 Who were Enrico Caruso and Luciano Pavarotti?

3 Why did Mussolini's government build the town Cinecittà?

4 Why were 'Spaghetti Westerns' made in Italy?

5 Where is Italy's most important film festival?

8

1 Why did explorers in the fifteenth and sixteenth centuries want to find a route across the sea to China?

2 Which explorer believed that Columbus's discovery was not in Asia?

3 Which inventor was also a painter and scientist?

4 What did Galileo believe about the Earth and the sun? What happened to him as a result of his ideas?

5 Who won the Nobel Prize for Physics in 1938 for his work on the first nuclear reactor?

9

1. What is the name of Internazionale's football stadium and why has it got this name?
2. What is the name of Italy's most important professional football league? How many teams play in this league?
3. Which Italian car designer has won more Formula 1 races than any other car-maker?
4. What mountains does the *Giro d'Italia* cycling race always travel through?
5. Which Italian water sport team won silver medals at the 2012 London Olympics?

10

1. Why did a large number of Italians go to the USA in 2013?
2. What food technology machines does Italy sell abroad?
3. What were three of the new inventions in technology and medicine at The Year of Italian Culture in the USA?
4. Which Italian company is making an exciting new superbike?
5. How are Italian families changing?

Glossary

1 ***Europe*** (page 5)
the large area of land that is between Asia and the Atlantic Ocean

2 ***divided*** – *to divide something* (page 5)
to keep two or more areas or parts of something separate

3 ***region*** (page 5)
a large area of land

4 ***proud*** (page 5)
feeling happy about your achievements, your possessions, or people who you are connected with

5 ***design*** (page 5)
the process of deciding how something will be made, how it will work, or what it will look like, or the study of this process. Someone whose job is to do this is a *designer*.

6 ***financial success*** (page 5)
the fact that you are making a lot of money

7 ***architecture*** (page 5)
the particular styles of buildings

8 ***passion*** (page 5)
something that you enjoy very much and are very interested in

9 ***population*** (page 5)
the number of people who live in a particular area

10 ***autonomous*** (page 5)
an autonomous state, region, or organization is independent and has the right to govern itself

11 ***volcano*** (page 6)
a mountain that forces hot gas, rocks, ash and melted rock called lava into the air through a hole in the top. An *active* volcano is likely to *erupt* – explode and pour out fire – at any time.

12 ***team*** (page 6)
a group of people who play a game or sport against another group

13 ***climate*** (page 7)
the climate of a place or country is the type of weather it has

14 ***border*** (page 8)
the official line that separates two countries or regions
15 ***grove*** (page 8)
a group of trees that are arranged in lines
16 ***rice*** (page 8)
a food consisting of small white or brown seeds that are eaten cooked
17 ***rock*** (page 8)
a large piece of the hard solid substance that forms part of the Earth's surface. An area of land with a lot of *rocks* is described as *rocky*.
18 ***sandy*** (page 9)
covered with *sand* – a pale brown substance formed from very small pieces of rock
19 ***buried*** – *to bury something or someone* (page 10)
to cover something with a layer or pile of something
20 ***protect*** – *to protect someone or something* (page 11)
to keep someone or something safe
21 ***species*** (page 11)
a plant or animal group whose members all have the same general features
22 ***race*** (page 12)
a competition that decides who is the fastest at doing something
23 ***earthquake*** (page 14)
a sudden shaking movement of the ground
24 ***myth*** (page 15)
an ancient traditional story about gods, magic and heroes
25 ***dome*** (page 16)
a roof shaped like the top half of a ball
26 ***monument*** (page 16)
a structure that is built in a public place in order to celebrate an important person or event
27 ***fountain*** (page 16)
a decoration for gardens and streets in which a stream of water is sent up into the air
28 ***powerful*** (page 17)
able to influence or control what people do or think

29 ***museum*** (page 17)
a building where valuable and important objects are kept for people to see or study

30 ***sculpture*** (page 17)
a solid object that someone makes as a work of art by shaping a substance such as stone, metal or wood. An artist who makes sculptures is called a *sculptor*.

31 ***chariot*** (page 17)
a vehicle with two wheels and no roof that was pulled by horses in races and battles in ancient times

32 ***politics*** (page 18)
the ideas and activities involved in getting power in an area or officially controlling and managing it. Someone who has a job in politics is called a *politician*.

33 ***emperor*** (page 18)
a man who rules an *empire* – a number of countries that are ruled by one person or government

34 ***arch*** (page 18)
a shape or structure with straight sides and a curved top

35 ***fresco*** (page 19)
a picture that is painted onto wet plaster on a wall, for example in a church

36 ***composer*** (page 21)
someone who *composes* – writes – music. For example, for an *opera* – a type of play that is performed by singers and an orchestra.

37 ***way*** (page 22)
a method for doing something

38 ***ruler*** (page 23)
someone who *rules* – controls – a country or region

39 ***cuisine*** (page 23)
a particular style of cooking

40 ***movement*** (page 24)
a group of people who work together in order to achieve a particular aim

41 ***fast food*** (page 24)
food that is made and served very quickly, and that you can take away with you

42 ***stir*** – *to stir something* (page 26)
to move food or a liquid around using a spoon or other object

43 ***course*** (page 26)
one of the parts of a meal

44 ***grilled*** – *to grill something* (page 26)
to cook something by putting it close to great heat above or below it

45 ***garlic*** (page 26)
a round white vegetable that is made up of sections. You use the sections in cooking in order to give the food a strong flavour

46 ***dish*** (page 26)
food that has been prepared and cooked in a particular way

47 ***grape*** (page 27)
a small green or purple fruit that grows in bunches on a plant called a vine and that is often used for making wine

48 ***mushroom*** (page 27)
a small white or brown fungus – a type of plant without leaves, flowers or green colour that grows in wet conditions. *Mushrooms* have a short stem and a round top and are often eaten as a vegetable.

49 ***republic*** (page 30)
a country that is not ruled by a king or queen

50 ***historian*** (page 31)
someone who studies history

51 ***invaded*** – *to invade somewhere* (page 32)
to take or send an army into another country to get control of it

52 ***religion*** (page 33)
a particular system of beliefs in a god or in gods

53 ***pope*** (page 33)
a leader of the Roman Catholic Church

54 ***destroyed*** – *to destroy something* (page 34)
to damage or harm something so severely that it cannot exist as it was before

55 ***controlled*** – *to control someone or something* (page 35)
to have the power to make decisions about what happens in a situation

56 ***trader*** (page 35)
someone who *trades* – buys and sells – things

57 ***well-educated*** (page 35)
a *well-educated* person has received a good education and has a lot of knowledge

58 ***inventor*** (page 35)
someone who has *invented* – designed and created – something that did not exist before. A new thing that has been *invented* is called an *invention.*

59 ***prime minister*** (page 36)
the political leader in countries such as the UK that are governed by a parliament

60 ***leader*** (page 37)
someone who is in charge of a group, organization, or country

61 ***relief*** (page 39)
a design or sculpture consisting of a raised surface on a flat background

62 ***figure*** (page 39)
the shape of a person's body

63 ***portrait*** (page 43)
a painting or drawing of a person

64 ***genius*** (page 43)
someone who is much more intelligent or skilful than other people

65 ***aristocrat*** (page 44)
a member of the highest class of society, who usually has money, land, and power

66 ***down-to-earth*** (page 45)
realistic and practical

67 ***landscape*** (page 45)
a painting of an area of land

68 ***literature*** (page 45)
stories, poems and plays, especially those that are considered to have value as art

69 ***prose*** (page 47)
ordinary written language such as in a novel or story. Another kind of writing is *poetry* – writing that uses beautiful or unusual language and is arranged in lines that have a particular beat and often rhyme – end with a similar sound. A piece of *poetry* is called a *poem*, and someone who writes poems is called a *poet.*

70 ***plague*** (page 49)
a disease that spreads quickly and usually ends in death

71 ***performed*** – *to perform* (page 51)
to do something in front of an audience in order to entertain them. An occasion when someone does this is called a *performance*.

72 ***detective*** (page 52)
a police officer whose job is to try to discover information about a crime

73 ***director*** (page 52)
someone whose job is to tell the actors and technical staff who are involved in a film, play, or programme what to do

74 ***published*** – *to publish something* (page 52)
to produce many copies of a book, magazine, or newspaper for people to buy

75 ***drama*** (page 54)
something unusual or exciting that happens

76 ***costume*** (page 54)
clothes that the actors wear in a play or film

77 ***tenor*** (page 54)
a man who sings the higher range of musical notes

78 ***explorer*** (page 58)
someone who travels to a place that other people do not know much about in order to find out what is there

79 ***voyage*** (page 60)
a long journey, especially on a ship

80 ***the Caribbean*** (page 60)
the islands in the Caribbean Sea and the countries that surround it. The region is southeast of the Gulf of Mexico and the North American mainland, east of Central America, and north of South America.

81 ***discovered*** – *to discover something* (page 60)
to find something that was hidden or that no one knew about before. Something that is *discovered* is called a *discovery*.

82 ***heresy*** (page 62)
a belief that is considered wrong because it is very different from what most people believe, or because it opposes the official beliefs of a religion

83 ***the nervous system*** (page 63)
the system of *nerves* – fibres in your body that carry messages to and from your brain – that control your body and your mind

84 ***nuclear reactor*** (page 63)
a machine used for producing nuclear energy, usually in the form of electricity

85 ***manager*** (page 65)
someone whose job is to organize and train a sports team

86 ***league*** (page 65)
an organized group of teams or players who compete against each other

87 ***championship*** (page 66)
a competition to find the best player or team in a sport or game

88 ***circuit*** (page 66)
a track that cars, bicycles etc race around

89 ***medal*** (page 69)
a small flat piece of metal that you are given for winning a competition or for doing something very brave

90 ***fencing*** (page 69)
the sport of fighting with a light thin sword

91 ***water polo*** (page 69)
a game that is played in water by two teams of seven players who get points by throwing a ball into the other team's goal

92 ***gymnastics*** (page 69)
a sport in which you perform physical exercises that involve bending and balancing

93 ***event*** (page 70)
an organized occasion such as a party or sports competition

94 ***Ministry of Foreign Affairs*** (page 70)
the government department that deals with a country's relations with other countries

95 ***embassy*** (page 70)
a group of officials who represent their government in a foreign country, or the building where they work

96 ***promote*** – *to promote something* (page 70)
to attract people's attention to something, for example by advertising

97 ***robot*** (page 71)
a machine that can do work by itself, often work that humans usually do

98 ***bone*** (page 71)
one of the hard parts that form the frame inside your body

99 ***birth rate*** (page 73)
the official number of babies born in a particular year or place

Useful Phrases

shop till they drop – *to shop till you drop* (page 22)
to spend a lot of time shopping and buying a lot of things until you are very tired

in other words (page 28)
used for introducing a simpler way of saying something

a part to play (page 33)
someone who has or is given *a part to play* in an event or situation is involved in influencing its development

made fun of – *to make fun of someone or something* (page 47)
to make jokes about someone or something in an unkind way

opened the eyes of – *to open someone's eyes to something* (page 51)
to make someone realize the truth about a situation

reached for the stars – *to reach for the stars* (page 62)
if you *reach for the stars* you try to achieve a very difficult aim

in a row (page 67)
if something happens a number of times *in a row*, it happens one time after another, without anything different happening in between

coming up with – *to come up with something* (page 71)
to think of something such as an idea or plan

kept the company going – *to keep something going* (page 73)
to do what is needed to make sure that something continues to exist or happen

look up to – *to look up to someone or something* (page 74)
to admire and respect someone or something

Exercises

Welcome to Italy

Which of these things does *Welcome to Italy* talk about? Tick the boxes.

art	☐	cars	☐	coffee	☐	fashion	☐
ice cream	☐	language	☐	mountains	☐	sport	☐

Geography, Climate and Environment

Match a place (1–12) to what it is famous for (a–l).

1	The Alps	a	The Italian Riviera.
2	The Po Valley	b	The highest active volcano in Europe.
3	The Apennine Mountains	c	Many different animals and birds.
4	The Ligurian Sea	d	They divide Italy from other European countries.
5	Basilicata and Calabria	e	Glaciers and ibex.
6	The Strait of Messina	f	Potatoes, rice and wheat.
7	Mount Etna	g	Stromboli.
8	Mount Vesuvius	h	They are 1,500 kilometres long.
9	The Aeolian Islands	i	It divides Italy from the island of Sicily.
10	Sicily	j	Rocky coasts and short sandy beaches.
11	Stelvio National Park	k	It buried two towns when it erupted in AD 79.
12	Grand Paradise National Park	l	It gets a lot of sun.

Cities and Architecture

Read the following statements about Italy. Write *T* (True) or *F* (False).

1 Rome has been there for more than 2,000 years. *T*
2 Today, the Pantheon is a church.
3 The Barcaccia Fountain is at the top of the Spanish Steps in Rome.
4 The Medici family lived in the Madama Palace in Rome.
5 People often throw money into the Trevi Fountain because they want to come back to Rome.
6 The Colosseum was the centre of Roman politics.
7 Aqueducts brought water into the ancient city of Rome.
8 Rome has nearly one thousand churches.
9 The Ponte Vecchio is a bridge across the River Arno in Florence.
10 Pisa is famous for its Tower.
11 Giacomo Puccini lived in Pisa.
12 Lucca's historic festival is called the Palio.
13 There are more than one hundred islands in Venice.
14 Milan is Italy's largest city.

Food and Drink

Complete the descriptions with the words in the box.

anchovies ~~*colazione*~~ espresso pesto
saffron *secondo* starter truffle

1 The first meal of the day is the *colazione* .
2 For a .... Italians often eat cold meat or a salad.
3 A .... is usually a dish of meat or fish.
4 Coffee with no milk is called ....
5 You can pay a lot of money for a ....
6 .... is yellow and it's very expensive.
7 You use nuts, basil and olive oil to make ....
8 .... are small dried fish.

A Short History

Put the events in the order that they happened.

- **a** Garibaldi and others brought the city-states into one country. [ ]
- **b** Italy became a member of the European Union. [ ]
- **c** Julius Caesar became ruler. [ ]
- **d** Mussolini became the leader of Italy. [ ]
- **e** People started to move from the south to the north of Italy and from the countryside to the cities. [ ]
- **f** The Etruscans lived around the River Tiber. [*1*]
- **g** The Renaissance started in Florence and other cities. [ ]
- **h** The Roman Empire divided into east and west. [ ]
- **i** The Roman Republic grew to rule Italy. [ ]
- **j** There started to be city-states in Italy. [ ]

Art, Literature, Music and Film

Match the sentence beginnings on the left to the correct endings on the right.

- **1** Roman mosaics were used
- **2** The Medici family
- **3** Some of Botticelli's paintings
- **4** Michelangelo Buonarroti
- **5** Canaletto
- **6** The Latin writer Livy
- **7** The poet Virgil
- **8** Dante is sometimes called
- **9** *Commedia dell'arte*
- **10** Luigi Pirandello
- **11** La Scala in Milan
- **12** Luciano Pavarotti
- **13** Cinecittà

- **a** painted a lot of landscapes of Venice.
- **b** died before he finished *The Aeneid*.
- **c** wrote *History of Rome*.
- **d** is a type of theatre.
- **e** is Italy's most famous opera house.
- **f** on walls and floors.
- **g** was a very popular tenor.
- **h** were painted for the Medici family.
- **i** painted a fresco in the Sistine Chapel.
- **j** paid painters and sculptors to work for them.
- **k** won the Nobel Prize for Literature.
- **l** 'the father of the Italian language'.
- **m** is the home of Italian cinema.

Explorers, Inventors and Scientists

Complete the descriptions with the names in the box.

Christopher Columbus Enrico Fermi Galileo Galilei
Maria Montessori Marco Polo ~~Giovanni da Verrazano~~
Amerigo Vespucci Leonardo da Vinci

1 *Giovanni da Verrazano* explored the coast of North America.
2 The first design for a helicopter was drawn by ....
3 .... travelled to China by land.
4 .... landed in South America.
5 .... sailed to the Caribbean.
6 .... had problems with the Catholic Church.
7 .... had some interesting new ideas about education.
8 .... won the Nobel Prize for Physics.

Sport

Read the following statements about Sport. Write *T* (True) or *F* (False).

1 The Italian football team plays in green shirts. *F*
2 Giuseppe Meazza scored thirty-three goals for Italy. ☐
3 Juventus' new stadium has more than forty thousand seats. ☐
4 Enzo Ferrari started to make cars in 1847. ☐
5 The *Giro d'Italia* is a car race. ☐
6 Armin Zöggler is a top skier. ☐

Vocabulary: History and Geography

Replace the underlined words with the words in the box.

border chariot climate earthquake emperor
museum population ~~regions~~ republic volcano

1 There are a number of different ~~reasons~~ *regions* in Italy.

2 The Trevi Fountain shows Neptune driving his car through the water.

3 The Roman <u>Empire</u> ended in 49 BC.

4 The biggest <u>city</u> in Italy is Mount Etna.

5 There are a lot of sculptures in the Roman National <u>Palace</u>.

6 There was a big <u>war</u> in Messina and Reggio di Calabria in 1908.

7 The Alps form the <u>break</u> between Italy and some other European countries.

8 The <u>position</u> of Rome is nearly three million.

9 Augustus was the first <u>king</u> of Rome.

10 The <u>city</u> of Sicily has got drier and drier.

Vocabulary: Famous places

Complete the sentences with the names of the places in the box.

Arno Colosseum Coverciano ~~Garda~~ Milan Pantheon San Carlo Theatre Siena Tyrrhenian Venice

1 Lake ....*Garda*.......... is one of the lakes in the north of Italy.
2 The .... Sea is to the west of Italy.
3 The .... is an old Roman temple in Rome.
4 Gladiators fought in the ....
5 The river that goes through Florence is called the ....
6 The best place to go shopping in Italy is probably ....
7 There is a Gothic cathedral in ....
8 Europe's oldest opera house is the .... in Naples.
9 Italy's most important film festival is in ....
10 The National Football Museum is in ....

Vocabulary: Art and architecture

Match the words on the left to the descriptions on the right.

1	dome	a	a man who sings the higher notes in opera
2	sculpture	b	a picture that was painted on wet plaster
3	fountain	c	a picture of a person
4	monument	d	a roof shaped like the top of a ball
5	fresco	e	a solid object often made of stone
6	portrait	f	a public structure to celebrate an important person or event
7	landscape	g	a decoration which uses water
8	poetry	h	a picture of the countryside
9	director	i	the person who tells people what to do in a film
10	tenor	j	language in lines and with a beat

Vocabulary: Food and drink

Complete the sentences with the words or phrases in the box.

cuisine garlic grape grill mushroom ~~rice~~ stir

1 ......*Rice*...... is small white or brown seeds that you can cook.
2 A special type of cooking is called a ....
3 When you cook something over or under great heat, you .... it.
4 .... is a small white vegetable with a very strong flavour.
5 When you move food or drink around with a spoon, you .... it.
6 A .... is a small white or brown fungus.
7 A .... is a small green or purple fruit.

Vocabulary: Anagrams

Write the letters in the correct order to make words from the book.

1	DOPRU	*proud*	feeling happy about your achievements
2	EGORV		a group of trees arranged in lines, usually to grow fruit
3	CEOPRTT		to keep someone or something safe
4	PROALITC		from the hottest parts of the world
5	CEEIPSS		a group of plants or animals
6	CEMOOPRS		a person who writes music
7	ADEINV		to send an army into another country
8	DEORSTY		to damage something badly
9	EGINSU		a very intelligent or skilful person
10	AEGLPU		a very dangerous disease which kills many people
11	CDEEEITTV		a police officer who tries to find information about crimes
12	CEFGINN		a sport with a thin sword

Grammar: prepositions

Complete the sentences with the correct preposition: *at, by, during, from, in, on* or *with.*

1 In Rome, culture was destroyed ....*during*.... the Dark Ages.
2 The Colosseum was built .... the Emperor Vespasian.
3 A sonnet is a poem .... fourteen lines.
4 Michelangelo painted a fresco .... the Sistine Chapel.
5 Risotto rice comes .... the Po Valley.
6 In the past most people ate lunch .... home.
7 Portofino is .... the Ligurian coast.

Grammar: passives

Complete the sentences with the verbs in the box in the correct past or present passive form.

~~build~~ cook destroy drink eat finish grow make

1 Palaces *were built* around the Piazza Navona in Rome for the pope and cardinals.
2 The Colosseum took a long time to build, and it .... in AD 80.
3 The best Italian food .... by Italians in Italy.
4 For many Italians lunch .... at home with the family.
5 Cappuccino .... at breakfast.
6 A lot of risotto rice .... in the Po Valley.
7 Gorgonzola cheese .... in Lombardy.
8 Across Europe, culture .... during the Dark Ages.

Grammar: connectives

Complete the sentences with the correct word: *how, where, when, which, who* or *why*.

1 The volcano Vesuvius buried the towns of Pompeii and Herculaneum *when* it erupted in AD 79.
2 Michelangelo is one of the famous artists .... worked in Florence and Rome during the Renaissance.
3 There is a 4,200 metre wall around the medieval town of Lucca, ... was built in the sixteenth century.
4 Naples is the city .... pizza was first made.
5 Nobody knows exactly .... Ovid was sent away from Rome.
6 When we look at the centuries of Italian art we can see .... it has changed over time.
7 The Grand Paradise National Park is a place .... you can see glaciers as well as ibex and many other animals.

Macmillan Education
4 Crinan Street
London N1 9XW
A division of Macmillan Publishers Limited
Companies and representatives throughout the world

ISBN 978-0-230-47015-6
ISBN 978-0-230-47014-9 (with CD edition)

Written by Coleen Degnan-Veness
The author has asserted her right to be identified as the author of this work in accordance with the Copyright, Designs and Patents Act 1988.
First published 2015

Designed by Carolyn Gibson
Map by Peter Harper
Cover photographs by Alamy/Marc Hill (front-bl); Alamy/Travelshots.com/Peter Phipp (front-tl); Corbis/Ocean/Reggie Casagrande/145 (front-r).
Picture Research by Kevin Brown.

The Author and publishers would like to thank the following for permission to reproduce their photographs: Alamy/blickwinkel p13(deer), Alamy/FineArt p44, Alamy/Paul Harris p13(bear), Alamy/HERA FOOD p24(cheese), Alamy/imageBROKER p12, Alamy/Mill Collection p61, Alamy/Sabine Lubenow p22, Alamy/PAINTING p50, Alamy/Alexander Perepelitsyn p41(mr), Alamy/PRISMA ARCHIVO p34(tr), Alamy/speedpix p66, Alamy/WILDLIFE GmbH p13(marmot); **ChinaFotoPress**/ChinaFotoPress via Getty Images p72(t); **Corbis** pp4-97(page icon-b), 21, Corbis/Susan Brooks-Dammann/Westend61 p27(br), Corbis/Christian Charisius/Reuters p56(tl), Corbis/Jerry Kobalenko/All Canada Photos p68(skating), Corbis/Sonja Pacho p73(tr), Corbis/Trish Punch/Design Pics p40, Corbis/Bernd Zoller/imageBROKER p13(eagle), Corbis/Radius Images p17, Corbis/Vittoriano Rastelli p38, Corbis/ZUMA p53(t); **Getty Images** p25(pasta), Getty Images/Pilar Azaña Talán p7(t), Getty Images/Allsport p68(luge), Getty Images/The Bridgeman Art Library/Peter Jackson p33, Getty Images/The Bridgeman Art Library/Musee National du Bardo, Le Bardo, Tunisia p46, Getty Images/DEA/G. CAPPELLI p13(wolf), Getty Images/DEA/A. DAGLI ORTI/De Agostini p30, Getty Images/DEA PICTURE LIBRARY p62(tr), Getty Images/DEA PICTURE LIBRARY/De Agostini p36, Getty Images/Digital Vision/David Madison p68(bobsleigh), Getty Images/Digital Vision/Karl Weatherly p68(skiing), Getty Images/Historic Map Works p59(t), Getty Images/The Image Bank/Chris Hepburn title page, Getty Images/Jupiterimages p63(tl), Getty Images/Laura Lezza p70, Getty Images/Ericka McConnell p29, Getty Images/Valerio Pennicino p65, Getty Images/Valerio Pennicino/Stringer p64, Getty Images/Photolibrary/Paul Poplis p25(salad), Getty Images/Polka Dot RF p49(mr), Getty Images/Universal Images Group/Leemage p48, Getty Images/Barbara Zanon p55; **Image Source** pp18(tr), 56(br); **Photo Alto** pp8(br), 26(ml); **Photodisc** pp25(olives), Photodisc/Getty Images p74(tr); **Thinkstock**/Dorling Kindersley p32(t), Thinkstock/iStock/edevansuk p13(fox), Thinkstock/iStock/**Kyslynskyy** p13(boar), Thinkstock/iStock/Jpiks1 p18, Thinkstock/iStock/MicheleBoiero p13(ibex), **Thinkstock**/iStock/marcoscisetti p9(br), Thinkstock/iStock/Paolo74s p25(polenta), Thinkstock/iStock/rz_design p10, Thinkstock/iStock/sborisov pp15(t), 20, Thinkstock/Photodisc/Jack Hollingsworth p24, Thinkstock/Wavebreak Media p5(mr).

Printed and bound in Thailand

without CD edition

2020 2019 2018 2017 2016 2015
10 9 8 7 6 5 4 3 2 1

with CD edition

2020 2019 2018 2017 2016 2015
10 9 8 7 6 5 4 3 2 1